HOW TO STUDY THE BIBLE FOR YOURSELF

Hope you
enjoy this book
and more importantly
Hope you enjoy the learning
in the Bible
God Bless you alway

R

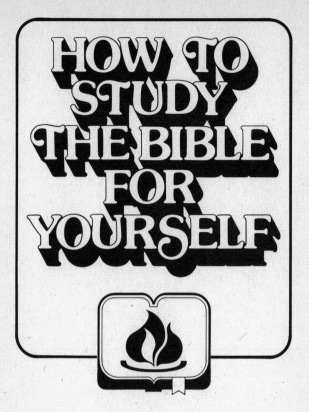

HOW TO STUDY THE BIBLE FOR YOURSELF

Tim LaHaye

HARVEST HOUSE PUBLISHERS
Eugene, Oregon 97402

HOW TO STUDY THE BIBLE FOR YOURSELF

Copyright © 1976
Harvest House Publishers
Eugene, Oregon 97402

Library of Congress Catalog Card Number: 76-5568
ISBN - 0 - 89081-021-4

Printed in the United States of America

*This book is dedicated to
the San Diego Charger football players
who met one season
for Bible study in our home.
Although it was a losing year
for the team, many of these men
won spiritual victories for themselves,
their wives and their several teammates
who received Christ.*

*Watching these young Christian athletes
begin to grow in their new found faith,
reminded me again of the need
for a simply written book
that shows a new Christian
how to study the Bible for himself.*

Contents

1

You Can Understand The Bible!

A seventeen year old young man went to church for the first time, because the shoe salesman who had led him to Christ told him he needed to learn more about the Savior he had just received. After the song service the minister said, "Turn to Second Timothy five twelve." The young convert turned to the first page of the Bible, which his friend had given him, and thumbed through Genesis, Exodus, Deuteronomy, Joshua and a number of other books but could not find Timothy. Turning to the table of contents he found Second Timothy was on page 325 but when he found that page number he was in the book of Joshua. Again looking into the table of contents he discovered there were two basic sections of the Bible and Second Timothy was in the second. By the time the young Christian had found the text the minister was finished with his sermon, needless to say he was embarrassed and a little befuddled.

Have you ever felt like that? Don't be discouraged, most new Christians start out the same way. From that discouraging beginning that young man developed a desire to know the Bible. Years later he became a famous preacher who, it is said, led one million people to Jesus Christ. In the later years of his life he founded a Bible Institute that today still trains over 1200 young people annually in the Word of God. His name was Dwight L. Moody. Few men have influenced Christianity more. But he would never have been an influence at all had he not been willing to study the Word of God for himself!

Although we don't know what method Moody used to study the Bible we do know he was not given much formal education, most of his Bible study was done on his own. The methods outlined in this book are probably similar to those he used. You too can be an effective servant of Christ—but only if you are willing to study the Bible for yourself.

Success or failure in the Christian life is dependent on how much of the Bible you get into your mind on a regular basis and how obedient you are to it. True, you can go to heaven knowing little more than John 3:16 and Romans 10:9 and 10, because God's marvelous gift of salvation is so free all you have to do to get it is to receive it by faith (John 1:12). But if you are ever going to be a happy, successful Christian it will be by regularly feeding on the Word of God and that takes work. The more you work at it the faster and better you will grow. You will find it is well worth the price you are called on to pay.

Jesus Christ gave the formula for success when He said, "If ye know these things, happy are ye if ye do them" (John 13:17). Happiness then is the result of knowing and doing the will of God as He has revealed it in the Bible. The problem with so many Christians is they have not spent the time learning the principles of the Bible so they don't even know what is expected of them. It is no wonder they do not enjoy all the blessings of the Christian life.

THE BIBLE WAS WRITTEN FOR PEOPLE

Unfortunately, most Christians have the idea they cannot understand the Bible. They think it was written for theologians or ministers so all they do is listen to "Bible scholars" lecture and preach or read books about the Bible, but spend very little time studying it for themselves. The thing that is so sad about this is that the Bible wasn't written for theologians, it was written for people just like you! For example, the Lord said through the apostle John, "I write unto you, *little children,* because your sins are forgiven you ... and because ye have known the Father" (1 John 2:12-13). Evidently then, "little children" or brand new Christians can understand the Bible. That means *you* can understand the Bible! Oh you may not be able to go down into the depths of

11

Bible truth the way the scholars do, and there will be things you won't understand, but you will find there is far more in the Scripture you can understand than what you cannot.

Once the fact that you can study the Bible for yourself really grips you, your Christian life will take on an entirely new dimension. I have watched new Christians and some old believers who had never been very excited about their Christian experience, really come to life by studying the Bible on their own. Through the years I've developed a very simple method of Bible study that has literally transformed the lives of those who have used it consistently. This book was written to help you study the Word of God and experience that same kind of transforming Christian experience.

There is one thing I must warn you—it takes work. A Greek mathematician once said, "There is no royal road to Geometry." This statement was made to a young student who wondered if there was an easier way of learning than study. As you know, there isn't, and the same is true for the Bible. In fact, it takes the hardest kind of work there is, thinking—but it is the only way it is ever learned. If you follow the program outlined in this book, it will be well worth it—you will develop a working knowledge of the Bible that will not only enrich your own spiritual life, it will enable you to serve Jesus Christ for years to come.

The idea for this method of study really came to me some years ago when I read an advertisement in a magazine, "Learn English in 15 minutes a day." Nothing had been harder for me in high school than English! This man showed me it could be mastered in just 15 minutes a day—and he is right. Actually you can master almost anything in 15 minutes a day if you do it long enough. This program will take 15 minutes a day for reading, another 15 minutes a day for study and some spare moments for learning. But by the end of three years you will have accomplished the following:

1. Read the Bible completely through.
2. Read the key books several times.
3. Accumulated the major principles, promises and commands.
4. Studied the most important chapters.
5. Learned several key verses.
6. Develop a working knowledge of the Bible.
7. Develop a lifetime habit of Bible study that will enrich your entire life.

The author assumes you regularly attend a Bible teaching church where you hear the Bible taught; this of course should be continued. Now we suggest you add the other four methods of Bible study—*reading, study, learning* and *thinking.* You will find the results well worth the time invested.

2

What Bible Study Will Do For You

Before we get into the mechanics of Bible study we should take a moment to see if it is really worth all the time you are going to invest in it. You have a legitimate right to ask, "What will 15 minutes a day spent reading the Bible and 15 minutes a day studying it do for me?" Consider the following:

1. It will make you a strong Christian. No one wants to be a weakling, physically or spiritually. The "young men" of 1 John 2:14 were no longer "children" but were "strong" and the Word of God abided in them and they overcame the wicked one. That means they had fed on the Word of God until they had grown strong enough in the faith that they were not continually defeated by sin and temptation. There is only one possible way to grow strong spiritually—reading and studying the Word of God.

Through the years I have watched thousands of Christians, some brilliant, others average, some with college backgrounds, others were scarcely educated, some had gone to Bible college and most did not. From each of those groups I have seen some remain continual babies while others grew strong in the Lord. The only thing they had in common was not their mutual gifts of education but whether or not they developed the habit of daily feeding their mind on the Word of God. Note that expression in verse 14 "you have overcome the wicked one," that takes spiritual strength that only comes from a study of the Word of God. Of the hundreds of spiritual failures I've counseled the thing they all had in common was an absence of the Word in their daily lives. All these failures (and consequent miseries) could have been avoided if they had learned to study the Word for themselves.

2. Assures us of Salvation. The first thing every young Christian needs is to be absolutely certain he is a Christian. Salvation is so marvelous, a free gift from a loving God, that it seems too good to be true. Consequently one of the first difficulties a new convert runs into after he has left the one who led him to Christ is entertaining doubts about his salvation. The *only source* of assurance is the Bible!

15

But what good is it to him if he doesn't read it for himself? The promises and guarantees of God are of little value between the covers of his Bible, Christians need them on the frontal lobes of their brain. And that's the reason the Bible was written. Listen to 1 John again, chapter 5, verse 13, "These things have I written unto you that believe on the name of the Son of God, *that ye may know that ye have eternal life.*"

The Christian that has an abiding assurance that he is a child of God and that God is *his* heavenly Father has the basis for a sound emotional life. The vast majority of those with fears, worries and other emotional foibles usually lack the assurance of salvation because they have been heeding their mind instead of reading their Bible. No man will be assured of God when limited to the thoughts of his mind, because as the Bible teaches, the concept of God does not come by thinking, but by the "wisdom of God"—the Bible (1 Cor. 1:21). If you would enjoy the assurance of your salvation then begin to study the Word of God regularly—it is the only place you will find it.

3. Gives us confidence and power in prayer. Now that you are a Christian you can talk to your heavenly Father about anything you have on your heart. But how do you know He is listening? Because He says so in His Word—in many places. 1 John 5:14, 15 teaches that we can pray in "confidence" that He hears us. In John 15:7 our Lord promised "If ye abide in me, and my words abide in you, ye shall ask what ye will, and it shall be done unto you." That means that Bible study (which is how His words abide in us) gives us power in prayer, because as we study His Word we become acquainted with His will and consequently learn how to pray.

Confucius was once asked by one of his students, "Does it help to pray for our sins?" To which he is said to have replied, "I am not sure but it can't hurt to try." That is no help at all! Only the Bible teaches that God answers prayer—the Bible-taught Christian enjoys that confidence.

4. Cleansing from Sin. Lady Macbeth was not the first to cry out in anguish of soul because of the guilt consciousness of her sin. This is a universal problem and like her, billions of people have no idea where to go for cleansing. This should never bother a Bible-taught Christian because as our Lord said, "Now ye are clean through the word which I have spoken unto you" (John 15:3). The Word of God has a cleansing effect upon the believer. Our Lord prayed, "Sanctify them through thy truth; thy word is truth" (John 17:17). Somehow the Word of God has a cleansing effect on the Christian who studies it.

A father was once asked by his son to explain how the Word of God cleansed a person. Instead of answering he asked his son to take a wicker basket down to the lake and bring him a basketful of water. The lad tried several times, but before he got back to where his dad was, the basket was empty. In frustration he complained to his father, "It's impossible, before I get it here the water has all run out." The father then called the boy's attention to how clean the basket was and said, "that is how the Word of God cleanses the believer as it passes through his mind." How do we know that our sins are forgiven? The Bible says, "If we confess our sins, he is faithful and just to forgive us our sins, and to cleanse us from all unrighteousness" (1 John 1:9). What encouragement it gives the soul to know that he is faithful in the work of cleansing!

As a young Christian, you need to know what is sin and what isn't. God has not left you to your own judgment. He says, "Wherewithal shall a young man cleanse his way? By taking heed thereto according to thy word" (Psalm 119:9). Studying the Bible will cleanse you from sin and warn you of sin.

When I was a young Christian, I asked a visiting minister to sign my Bible, which he did, but he also added a note that is very perceptive, "This book will keep you from sin or sin will keep you from this book."

5. It gives joy. One of the blessings of the Christian life is joy, but often times that joy is stifled by the problems of life. Our Lord said, "These things have I spoken unto you, that my joy might remain in you, and that your joy might be full" (John 15:11). If you read the writings of men or look at the problems that surround you, joy will turn to fear, dread or sometimes depression.

During a recessionary period I attended a meeting of the Board of Trustees. As I listened to the men talk you would think the Lord had gone out of business—all they did was forecast gloom, doom and despair. I asked, "What have you men been reading lately?" They replied, "*The Wall Street Journal, U.S. News and World Report, The San Diego Union,* etc." I then said, "You've

18

been reading the wrong material!'' It is the Word of God that puts joy in your heart, regardless of the circumstances.

6. It produces peace. One of the supernatural evidences of the Christian life is peace in one's heart when the circumstances of life call for worry and anxiety. Now that you have received Christ as your Savior and Lord you have a right to expect to be different and your friends are justified in expecting to see that difference. When a supernatural power, like the Holy Spirit comes to live in the life of a natural human being, he will be different. That difference is primarily shown in our emotions that are characterized by peace in the face of difficulties. But if the Word of God does not ''dwell in you richly'' by reading and study, it will not produce the ''peace'' that should characterize your life.

Jesus Christ said, ''These things have I spoken unto you, that in me ye might have peace. In the world ye shall have tribulation: but be of good cheer, I have overcome the world'' (John 16:33). What makes this statement of particular interest is that our Lord gave this message to His disciples just before the turmoil that resulted in His crucifixion. As His disciples faced this impending crisis, He wanted them to have *peace* through His Word. For almost two thousand years now God's people have fortified themselves for the crises of life by reading and studying the Bible. That's what God meant when He said, ''And let the peace of God rule in your hearts, to which also ye are called in one body; and be ye thankful'' (Col. 3:15). Peace is not automatic. We let it flood our hearts through filling our mind with the promises,

19

principles and faithfulness of God as taught in His Word. Many a Christian business man who reads the Wall Street Journal or Time magazine daily instead of his Bible becomes upset at monetary conditions, when all the time God wants to flood his heart with peace through the daily reading of His Word.

7. It guides us in making the decisions of life. Life is filled with decisions! Little ones, big ones and many in between. When the principles of God are well known to a Christian it simplifies the process of decision making. That's what is meant when the Scripture says, "Thy word is a lamp unto my feet, and a light unto my path" (Psalm 119:105). The principles of God serve as a guide in reaching decisions.

Today's "Situation Ethics" philosophy is a chaotic approach to life that produces much harm. It is far better to program Bible principles to live by into one's mind in advance of a crisis than to wait until emotions, passions and life pressures close in on you before deciding what to do. As the Lord himself said, "Blessed (happy) are they that hear the word of God, and keep it" (Luke 11:28). You can't keep what you have not heard! But as you fill your mind daily with the Word of God it will enlighten the dark paths of the future with divine guidance.

8. It enables you to articulate your faith. Most of the people you meet in life are ignorant of Bible concepts. Many of these have questions or doubts and need someone who knows the Bible to guide them. As God challenges us, "But sanctify the Lord God in your hearts, and be ready always to give an answer to every man that asketh you a reason of the hope that is in you, with meekness and fear'' (1 Peter 3:15). The only way you will be able to answer the questioner, scorner, or sincere seeker of truth is to be "ready always to answer" them by daily reading and studying the Word. A Navy lieutenant I counseled who claimed to have been a Christian eleven years said, "I never have an opportunity to share my faith with anyone." It seemed incredible to me that a man stationed aboard an aircraft carrier with 3000 other men couldn't find someone to share Christ with, but I ignored his comment and started him on a Bible reading, studying and learning program. Two months later when he came in for his weekly check-up he told about leading his first soul to Christ. Then he reminded me of his previous comment and said, "My problem wasn't lack of opportunity; I just didn't know what to do when one came along. Now my mind is so filled with the Word of God I'm sharing it all the time. Before I started studying the Bible I just didn't know what to say." That young man's experience could be multiplied many times—you cannot communicate what you do not know. Almost every Christian wants to be fruitful and effectively share Christ with others, but it is totally impossible without at least an elementary knowledge of the Word of God.

9. It guarantees your success! Everyone wants to be successful. That doesn't mean we all want riches or fame; you can have those without success. We all yearn to succeed in our chosen field of endeavor; that's why "How to" or "success oriented" books are so popular today. No one reads books on how to fail! Joshua 1:8 tells us, "This book of the law shall not depart out of thy mouth, but thou shalt meditate therein day and night, that thou mayest observe to do according to all that is written therein; for then thou shalt make thy way prosperous, and then thou shalt have good success." Note these words, "and then thou shalt have good success." Daily meditation (thinking) on the Word of God produces the success everyone desires. Certainly it did for Joshua. Many Christian businessmen have claimed that same promise and today testify to God's faithfulness.

Lest you think God's promise to Joshua an isolated one, we should look at the formula for happiness found in the first Psalm. "Blessed is the man who walketh not in the counsel of the ungodly, nor standeth in the way of sinners, nor sitteth in the seat of the scornful. But his delight is in the law of the Lord; and in his law doth he meditate day and night. And he shall be like a tree planted by the rivers of water, that bringeth forth its fruit in its season; its leaf also shall not wither; and whatsoever he doeth shall prosper" (Psalm 1:1-3). That kind of daily productivity comes from daily feeding one's mind on the Word of God.

Unfortunately, many Christians think they are "too busy" to refresh the mind each day on the Word of God. What they don't realize is that a daily quiet time costs them nothing in the long run for the rest of their day will be more successful than had they ignored their Bible. A brilliant neuro-surgeon in Atlanta claims, "The most important part of my day is the first thirty minutes after awaking, consequently I spend 20 minutes of it reading and studying the Word of God. It enriches the rest of my day." Try it, you'll like it!

3

How To Read The Bible

For all practical purposes, reading is the foundation of all learning. Someone has said, "If you can read you can learn anything." If you are going to learn the Bible, you will have to develop the habit of reading large portions of the scriptures. Bible study is essential to be a "workman approved unto God" (2 Timothy 2:15). But the foundation of that study must be reading. We shall distinguish between devotional reading and study reading. The latter shall be discussed at length in another chapter on "How to Study the Bible." But it has been my observation that unless a person has the regular habit of reading the Bible, he will never develop a regular study habit. In fact, it is usually the consistent practice of reading the Scriptures that inspires a person to become a student of the book. I have never met a person who enjoyed studying the Bible who had not first developed the habit of regular reading.

One of the advantages of reading the Bible is that the student doesn't get so bogged down in the complexities of verse or word analysis that he loses the overall purpose and meaning of the writer. These minute methods to study which will be covered later should not be attempted until the reader is acquainted with the main theme—and that is only possible by reading the whole book. Dr. G. Campbell Morgan, a popular Bible commentator of another generation, used to say he would not attempt to teach any book of the Bible until he first had read it fifty times. He felt it took that many readings to properly relate all of the parts to the whole.

To gain the most value from your reading consider carefully the following techniques.

1. Read daily. Daily Bible reading is to your spiritual life what daily eating is to your physical life. We are all familiar with the necessity of regular mealtimes, otherwise we skip meals or rush them, consequently their primary values are lost. Just as the body needs a regular feeding time to maintain its energy level, so the spiritual man must regularly be fed the Word of God. Job compared the two in 23:12 where he said, "Neither have I gone back from the commandment of his lips; I have esteemed the words of his mouth more than my necessary food."

Most people find that morning is the best time to read the word devotionally. It is easier to program Bible reading into your schedule in the morning because all you have to do is get up fifteen minutes earlier to get your 15 minute reading done. If you are a morning person, one who wakes up bright and alert, it is particularly advisable to do it then, for it gets your day off to a good start. If, however, you are like some of the rest of us, night people, or "nocturnalists" your brain isn't too swift early in the morning. We function best at night, consequently it might be advisable to do it after dinner or before retiring.

The biggest problem with setting your daily Bible reading (or quiet time) at night is that if you forget it or a change of schedule necessitates that you miss the regular time, it is difficult to work it in later. The most common time, early in the morning, provides ample substitute scheduling, if perchance the regular time must be skipped.

Whatever the time, it has been my observation that if you don't set one, your good intentions will never be realized and you will only occasionally read your Bible.

2. Set a regular reading time. How much time should I devote to reading the Bible each day? is a question I hear frequently. My answer depends on my appraisal of the seriousness and discipline of the individual. If I suspect they are good starters and poor finishers, I say "at least 5 minutes." I'd rather have them consistent at 5 minutes a day than nothing. But frankly, if you mean business with God and really want to develop a working knowledge of the Word, you had better plan on a minimum of 15 minutes daily.

When you think about it, that isn't too much. Most people spend that long reading the newspaper or watching newscasts on T.V., or spend that long unnecessarily on the telephone. In addition, we usually spend more time than that three times a day feeding our bodies.

Our three year program of providing you with a working knowledge of the Bible is based on at least 15 minutes reading and 15 minutes studying each day over a three year period. I don't see how the average person will ever develop an adequate knowledge of the Word on less.

Most of those who have followed this procedure indicated that after the first or second month they have developed the reading habit to the extent that frequently they become so engrossed with God's message to them they lose track of time and read much longer than the minimum 15 minutes.

3. Set a regular place. It will help your concentration and consistency if you set a regular place to do your 15 minutes or more daily reading. All speed reading experts recommend that reading be done in a sitting position and preferably at a desk, as it aids in concentration. Another thing it does is eliminate other visual distractions. The less you have on your desk besides your Bible while reading the better. Coming regularly to this "quiet place" helps establish the devotional mood.

4. Read with a pencil at hand. The biggest danger to devotional Bible reading is in letting your eyes run across the words and assuming you have read the material. Many Christians spend the allotted 15 minutes each day, follow their reading with prayer and assume they have had an effective quiet time. But if you asked them one hour later what they had read, they wouldn't have the foggiest idea. Their eyes read the words but their brain wasn't turned on.

The best way to dial your brain into a vital attitude is to pick up a pencil and be ready to receive a message from God. That very act makes you more alert and expectant as you read that God will communicate something to you today which you need to know. Another thing it does is assist your memory. An educator once said, "There is no learning without written duplication." When you see something special in your reading, write it down. Not only does this record it for handy review in the future, it also helps to cement the thought more forceably into your brain.

5. Read the Bible devotionally. The Bible is a living book written by a loving God to His children and it is "profitable" (practical). In it He provides basic principles, guidance and inspiration on how to live. It was written to people and because human nature hasn't changed in the years since its writing, it has a message for God's people today. More than a message, however, the Bible is true soul food.

Man is not just body, mind and emotions, as most humanists indicate, but he has a strong spiritual side to his nature also! That area of his being is indwelt at salvation as a "new creature" (2 Corinthians 5:17, "Therefore, if any man be in

28

Christ, he is a new creation; old things are passed away; behold all things are become new.'') and must be fed from that time on. Consequently, even when a person doesn't find anything special in his reading (and some days will be like that) there still is an aspect of spiritual benefit just in the reading, for it feeds this devotional or spiritual side of our being.

The best way to read the Word of God devotionally is to prayerfully ask Him for some message for today. Many times He will give you a thought that answers the hunger of your heart. Sometimes He will give you a blessing you will need later in the day. In either case it proves helpful to write it down as suggested above. Special care, however, should be taken to make sure the thought is true. We shall go into this in detail later, but a verse should never be lifted out of its setting to provide a special message today when by doing so it is in contrast to the sense of the whole passage. Remember, the Bible was written in paragraphs, not verses. The verse divisions were added about 1500 years after the Scripture was completed and although they are handy aids to finding special messages and teachings, it is dangerous for them to be lifted out of context. Since the Holy Spirit is the author of the Bible and since He is the one who inspires us with a devotional message from God as we read it, He will *never* lead us to use a portion of His word that is contrary to His will or in conflict with His original meaning.

Devotional reading provides that spiritual inspiration for daily living that every Christian needs and it is always based on the truth revealed in the Bible.

6. Keep a daily spiritual diary. The best single tool I have used or helped others to use to get the greatest blessing out of their devotional reading is to establish the habit of keeping a daily spiritual diary. When the idea of keeping a diary first came to me I rejected it because I'm not the diary keeping type. But as I wrote down my thoughts from God found in my daily Bible reading, it seemed to naturally fall into place. Since then I have shared it with hundreds of Christians who really wanted to deepen their spiritual lives and enrich their relationship to God. Many have testified that it has proven the most inspirational tool they have ever used.

A fancy diary or notebook is not necessary, an ordinary sheet of paper or a small 25 cent spiral notebook will suffice. Allowing a page per day, put the day of the week, the month and the day on top with space for the text to be read. In a Bible class I taught for 47 students who were required to keep a daily diary, I discovered 47 different formats when I collected them at the end of the term. Some were ornate and elaborate, others were simplicity itself. The important thing was they were done! On page 35 is a sample of the kind made available by Family Life Seminars. In the last chapter of this book are enough to last one month. You would be advised to use them and by that time either develop your own system or order additional copies.

WHAT TO INCLUDE
IN YOUR SPIRITUAL DIARY

As seen in the enclosed sample diary, there are five things that should be included in your diary.

1. God's message to you today. The first thing to look for is that special message from God for the day. Naturally, this will be influenced largely by the passage under study for that day and your own particular need at the time.

2. A promise from God. The Bible is filled with promises from God to His children. You won't find one in every passage, but they are so common you will locate one frequently. In many passages you will find several; for that reason you should select the best one from the three or four chapters you read that day. There are two things to consider in claiming promises, make sure they are universal promises and that they apply to you. Some are for Israel, some are for the people in the millennium and others are promised judgments on the wicked. The little chorus that used to be popular in Sunday School, "Every promise in the book is mine..." just isn't true. As a rule, the context will indicate clearly whether it is for you or someone else.

Another thing to keep in mind when looking for promises is, "Are there any conditions" to the promise? For example, a recent heresy has become quite popular in some circles based on the promise that God "is faithful and just to forgive us our sins and to cleanse us from all unrighteousness," according to 1 John 1:9. They suggest that anytime a Christian sins he is automaticaly forgiven. It is difficult for most of us to understand why those who hold this idea do not read the condition clearly stated in that verse which is *"If* we confess our sins He is faithful and just to forgive us our sins, and to cleanse us from all unrighteousness." We must confess our sins (admit to God they are wrong) or they will not be forgiven. Never claim a promise from God unless you are willing to meet the conditions listed. That is why you should always write down the conditions that precede a promise so you will know whether or not it is legitimate for you to claim.

3. A command to keep. The Bible is filled with commands for God's people to obey. These commands are for our good, the keeping of them both lengthens and enriches our lives. As you come upon them in your reading, you will be forced to select the most important for your life at that moment and enter it into your diary.

4. A timeless principle. One of the reasons the Bible is the greatest manual on human behavior ever written is because it contains thousands of timeless principles for daily living. These are divine insights that guide the believer and help program his mind in advance so that when decisions are to be made he doesn't have to go through an agonizing thought process to make a decision. Consider some samples:

"Whatsoever a man soweth that shall he also reap." "Humble yourselves under the mighty hand of God and He will exalt you." "Be not unequally yoked together with unbelievers."

Obeying these and many other timeless principles are what produce happiness and fulfillment in the lives of God's people. The last one listed above saved a printer I know over $40,000 of debts when offered a "good deal" by another printer who was not a Christian. One week after refusing to get involved with this unbeliever in a partnership the fraud he was almost a part of was revealed. Many Christians have saved themselved from an unfortunate marriage by applying the timeless principle in that verse. There are principles in the Bible on almost every subject in the world, by listing one in your daily diary each day you will have over 300 by the end of your first year.

5. Your application. As a practical tool in implementing the above "finds" in your daily reading, pick out one that is in the area of your greatest need and list how you intend to implement it into your daily life. For example, suppose your command for the day is "Husbands, love your wives, even as Christ also loved the church ..." (Ephesians 5:25). Pick some area where you know you have been selfish with your partner and write in a sentence how you plan to be more loving. By asking God's help you will find that not only will your spiritual life improve but the relationship with your wife will be enhanced.

This kind of simple but practical application to your life of the daily challenges you find in God's Word will definitely transform your life to the kind of growing, consistent Christian walk that every child of God needs. More will be said later about applying God's truth to your life.

REASONS FOR
KEEPING A SPIRITUAL DIARY

There are many reasons for keeping a daily spiritual diary; consider the following.

1. It provides a handy method for recording special daily insights from God's Word. Good intentions are fine, but unless you have an organized plan for implementing them you will never prove consistent in your devotional life, and without one there is little chance for spiritual maturity and success. But a handy spiritual diary kept near your Bible makes it easy to get off by yourself with a pencil and spend at least 15 profitable minutes with God each day.

2. It produces an attitude of expectancy. Unless you plan to enter something into a notebook or diary, your daily quiet time often becomes drudgery. Keeping a daily spiritual diary develops a mental attitude of expectancy that not only attunes your brain for diligent thought but helps with consistency by producing a spirit of anticipation that today you will hear from God.

3. It provides a handy check on regularity. In a glance you can tell just how consistent you are in your quiet time for the skipping of days is readily apparent. Many Christians think they are more consistent in their devotions than they really are, the daily spiritual diary will keep you honest.

4. It provides a handy review. One of the blessings in keeping a daily diary is that in a few minutes each week you can review the "cream" of your devotional reading for the week and month. This review further helps to cement the Word of God into your mind.

5. It provides an easy appraisal of spiritual growth. By the time you have kept a spiritual diary for three months you will be amazed at how much more mature you have

Daily Spiritual Diary

Week of _____ to _____

"I have desired the words of His mouth more than my necessary food."
Job 23:12

Sunday: Passage _____ Date _____

God's message to me today: _____

_____

A Promise from God	A Command to Keep	A Timeless Principle
_____	_____	_____
_____	_____	_____
_____	_____	_____

How does this apply to my life? _____

_____

Monday: Passage _____ Date _____

God's message to me today: _____

_____

A Promise from God	A Command to Keep	A Timeless Principle
_____	_____	_____
_____	_____	_____
_____	_____	_____

How does this apply to my life? _____

_____

Tuesday: Passage _____ Date _____

God's message to me today: _____

_____

A Promise from God	A Command to Keep	A Timeless Principle
_____	_____	_____
_____	_____	_____
_____	_____	_____

How does this apply to my life? _____

_____

Additional Comments _____

_____

_____

_____

Wednesday: Passage _____ Date _____
God's message to me today: _____
_____

A Promise from God   A Command to Keep   A Timeless Principle
_____   _____   _____
_____   _____   _____
_____   _____   _____

How does this apply to my life? _____
_____

Thursday: Passage _____ Date _____
God's message to me today: _____
_____

A Promise from God   A Command to Keep   A Timeless Principle
_____   _____   _____
_____   _____   _____
_____   _____   _____

How does this apply to my life? _____
_____

Friday: Passage _____ Date _____
God's message to me today: _____
_____

A Promise from God   A Command to Keep   A Timeless Principle
_____   _____   _____
_____   _____   _____
_____   _____   _____

How does this apply to my life? _____
_____

Saturday: Passage _____ Date _____
God's message to me today: _____
_____

A Promise from God   A Command to Keep   A Timeless Principle
_____   _____   _____
_____   _____   _____
_____   _____   _____

How does this apply to my life? _____
_____

become. At first you skim the surface with your findings but gradually you dig deeper into the meanings of the Word and it will produce greater challenges as you do so. It will also provide a blessing when you discover that some of the previous challenges are now a regular part of your life. Without this kind of record you may not realize that you are growing in grace and knowledge and in wisdom and stature with God.

4

Methods Of Bible Reading

There are four recommended methods for reading the Bible.

1. Read it by books. The books of the Bible were written either to individuals or groups of people, for that reason they should be read in their entirety. This way you keep in mind the overall message of the book and are less likely to wrest a text out of its context.

Many use the "hunt and peck" system. They open the Bible at random and hope they find something for the day. This method is better than nothing, but not much, and sometimes it is dangerous. The story is told of one person using the "hunt and peck" method, who opened to Matthew 27:5 "and Judas hanged himself." He then opened to another passage and discovered "Go and do likewise"; still a third "peck" produced the advice, "and what thou doest, do quickly." Such a discovery could be interpreted by the individual as a lack of love on God's part in not providing him better instruction for the day, when in reality it wasn't God's fault but his disastrous method of Bible reading. This will never happen when you read it by books. It would also be advisable to familiarize yourself with the purpose and theme of the book before you commence. This can usually be located in your Bible or in a copy of *Halley's Bible Handbook*. More will be said about this later.

2. Read it repeatedly. One of the best ways to get to know a book thoroughly is to read the entire book every day for thirty days; this, of course, is limited to those books containing four to six chapters. Most of the epistles can be read this way with great profit. By the thirtieth day you will really know that book. This method should probably not be employed until you have read the New Testament through at least once.

3. Read it by need. Your personal spiritual needs will often determine what you read. Particularly if you read it repeatedly. If a person lacks the assurance of salvation, I always recommend they read 1 John every day for thirty days. So far I have yet to find one plagued by feelings of eternal insecurity after thirty days of reading 1 John. Particularly if after the tenth day they begin compiling a list of the 27 things God wants us to know that are found in that little epistle. The entire book can easily be read in approximately 15 minutes. More details will be given on this in the next chapter.

4. Read it entirely. Every Christian should read the Bible all the way through, beginning with the New Testament. In the next chapter we shall discuss this in detail and offer a three year suggested reading program.

HOW TO BE CONSISTENT IN DAILY BIBLE READING

"Consistency thou art a gem" is a saying of a friend of mine who all but destroyed himself by inconsistency. Knowing the problem does not always guarantee a remedy. Doubtless more Christians have gone down the spiritual drain or failed to grow in their Christian lives through inconsistency in their daily devotional lives than any other one thing. As we have seen, it is absolutely essential to get into the Word daily, to keep fresh and filled with the Spirit, but unfortunately, only a small percentage of God's people have found this key.

Self-discipline is not the hallmark of this affluent age in which we live. But it has been my observation that self-discipline is the name of the game as far as success is concerned. Whether it is a Mickey Mantle whose three to five hours a night as a youngster hitting his father's right hand pitching and his grandfather's left hand pitching produced the greatest switchhitting baseball player of all time, or a Paul Anderson whose daily hours of weight-lifting made him the strongest man in the world, or Terry Bradshaw, a premier football quarterback, or Billy Jean King who has won 19 Tennis Championships at Wimbledon, discipline is the name of the game! Admittedly, they had talent but so do thousands of others in this world, but they added the discipline of practice to their talent and became established superstars.

The only difference in my analogy above and the success in the Christian life is that every Christian could be a super spiritual success *if* he would discipline himself to the daily quiet time we have outlined here and the implementation of God's principles into his life. Most of us could never be super athletes because that isn't the area of our talent, but all of us can be effective Christians. If you will pardon a personal illustration, I'll show you what I mean. With almost two million copies in print of my seven published books, many have asked why did I wait until I was almost forty years old before writing my first book. The answer is rather humbling, but true. It took me all those years to learn to discipline myself to the work of writing. I used to say, "I'm too busy to write, beside, who would read anything I wrote?" But that wasn't the real problem; I had to finally come to the place that writing was so important to me that it deserves at least one day of my life every week. Now it is no problem to be productive. Until you decide that your spiritual development is worth at least 15 minutes a day in the Word of God you will remain a mediocre Christian. Remember this, the potential is yours as a gift from God, what you do with it is up to you.

During the life of our Lord He had various kinds of people who showed an interest in Him. The Bible tells us that "many believed on Him," but little is heard of them. Others "came after Him," but when persecution and adversity arose they returned home. Still others said, "We would be thy disciples," and He said, "If any man will come after me, let him *deny himself,* and take up his cross *daily,* and follow me" (Luke 9:23). As is well known, He had only twelve disciples and another 120 like them who were devoted to the Savior. Isn't it interesting that the words "disciple" and "discipline" are so similar? You can't have the first without the second.

Dr. M. R. DeHaan, the late founder of the nationally aired program, "Radio Bible Class," once said, "To come to Christ costs nothing, to follow Christ costs something, but to serve Christ will cost you everything." I would not deceive you; there is a cost involved in spiritual growth and maturity. It is the time it takes to learn about God's principles from His Word and the submission of your life to them. However, the rewards and results are well worth the sacrifice they require.

A GUARANTEED FORMULA
FOR LEARNING SELF-DISCIPLINE

On the basis of many years spent in helping Christians, particularly men, who wanted to learn discipline in their daily devotional life, I can guarantee the following three-step formula for success. There is no way you can fail if you incorporate these steps.

1. Read when you feel like it; read when you don't. It would be unrealistic to suggest that every morning when you awake 15 minutes early, your brain will be 100% "on" and you will be eager to get into the Word. There will be mornings like that, and there will be some when you awake feeling like the rapture occurred and you have been left behind, particularly if you are a late night worker. But don't give in to the lackadaisical suggestion your mind offers that "if you don't feel like doing it, you won't get much out of it," or "it's better to wait until you have a hunger for Bible reading," or "you have to be in the right mood to receive a blessing." These are all lies of the devil or our deceitful mind!

If you wake up feeling drowsy or "dead," take a shower and get dressed before your quiet time. But put in your 15 minutes minimum reading time whether you feel like it or not! Some of the greatest quiet times I have had were when I prayed, "Heavenly Father, I feel lousy this morning and very honestly don't even want to read your Word. Forgive my carnal attitude, and open my mind that I may see wonderful things in your Word today, Amen." Years ago I heard a preacher say, "Read the Word when you feel like it and when you don't feel like it, read until you do." You will find that as you read your "feeling" will gradually change and you will get a special blessing from His Book.

2. Make a sacred vow with God. Ordinarily I do not challenge Christians to make vows to God, because the scripture says, "It is better that you should not vow than that you should vow and not pay" (Eccle. 5:5). But since it is so essential to maintain a daily reading of the Word, I make this one exception, because it has a long history of producing the consistency which I believe most Christians desire.

As a young minister I met a missionary whose personal life and consistency I greatly admired. When asked for "the secret of your success," he replied, "I never miss a daily time with God in prayer and Bible study." To my question, "How did you learn to be so consistent?" he replied, "Very simple; I made a sacred vow with God, *no Bible, no breakfast.*" He then explained that there were a few times in his schedule when he awakened late, or a child was sick or some emergency prohibited his time in the Word. But when that occurred he said, "I just skip breakfast. If I am too rushed to feed my soul, I am too busy to feed my body. Through the years I've only missed a few breakfasts because of my inability to feed my soul first." I have shared this vow with hundreds of people; many have made and kept it for years.

Recently I told that story during a Bible study in our home for San Diego Charger football players. Two weeks later one of the brilliant special team players told me he had made that vow during our closing prayer and had found it to be a tremendous help in bringing discipline into his spiritual life. Here is an extremely talented young man who had learned to discipline himself athletically, but needed a little mental handle like this to effect discipline in his devotional life.

Very simply, the vow is—*no Bible, no breakfast.* For those who need a scripture verse to verify everything they do, try Job 23:12, "Neither have I gone back from the commandment of his lips; I have esteemed the words of his mouth more than my necessary food." Evidently, Job had his own vow with God that sounds a lot like, *no Bible, no breakfast*.

3. Make no exceptions! The last part of the formula is very simple; make no exceptions. Once you give in the vow is broken and it becomes easy to repeat your inconsistency. The refusal to make exceptions is a fundamental requirement to consistency in anything. Alcoholics Anonymous have established for all to know that the only path to victory over the bottle is to *make no exceptions*. "That first drink proved my downfall," is a common wail of the AA member who wound up on skid row again.

Those who diet know this fundamental rule, as do joggers or self-disciplinarians in any field. I remember going three years without touching sweets, during which time I lost 40 pounds. Then I decided I could "handle my sweet tooth now," and took one piece of candy—then another and gained 15 pounds back before making that vow again. Even now I cannot diet and make exceptions—and neither can you or anyone else.

Right here I would like to issue you a challenge; try this formula for one year; make your vow, *no Bible, no breakfast;* allow for no exceptions and you will be a much more consistent and effective Christian in 365 days! Keeping this vow will change your life.

5

What To Read In The Bible

What to read in the Bible is as important as how to read, particularly for a young Christian. When I was a high school student I went to summer youth camp every year. It was there that many of the biggest spiritual decisions of my life were made, surrender of my will to Christ, surrender of my life to the ministry and many others. I thank God for the people who ran that camp, but I wish they had told me what to read in the Bible. Each year they would challenge us to read it every day and each year I would go home from camp determined to be consistent. All through high school I did the same thing, started at the beginning, like any other book and read Genesis. Fortunately I enjoy history so Genesis was a lark, then came Exodus and the work of Moses, but half way through that book I got bogged down in the sockets and tapestry of tabernacle construction and gave up—after about two months (that was before I had heard about no Bible, no breakfast).

It is too bad someone hadn't told me at that early age that as great as the Old Testament is, it was written largely to Israel and that age, and I am a New Testament Christian. As such I should have learned my way around the New Testament before working on the Old Testament. That should not be taken as an indication that the Old Testament is not important to the Christian; it is, particularly certain books, but it is much more important for Christians to understand the 27 books of the New Testament for they were written expressly to the Church (and the Christians in the church) for their edification.

Everything you need to know about God is found in the Bible. Everything you need to know to grow spiritually strong is found in the Bible. But as the next chapter will show, the Bible is not just an ordinary book; it is a library of 66 books and just like any library, you have to go to the right section to get what you need. The following suggested reading schedule is designed to help streamline the learning process for a young Christian so that he may concentrate on those books that have the answers to his greatest need. If you follow the schedule in this chapter, you will read the most important books for you to know several times the first year, the New Testament through twice and by the third year you will have read the entire Bible. They are listed in the order that I consider most important. Included with each is a brief reason why they are considered so important.

1. Read 1st John seven times. The primary need of every new Christian is the assurance of his salvation. I have observed there is little spiritual growth possible until once he settles the fact that he is an eternal child of God, that what Jesus Christ did on Calvary's cross was to redeem him from his past sins forever and adopt him into the eternal family of God. This truth is so marvelous and so contradictory to human intuition, intelligence and understanding that it *only* comes through the Word of God. If we waited until we were good enough or "became worthy" to be assured of eternal life, none would have it. The only way to gain that assurance is through the Word of God and of all the 66 books of the Bible only the little epistle of 1st John was written for that express purpose. The author admitted his purpose in chapter 5 verse 13 by saying, "These things have I written unto you that believe on the name of the Son of God, that ye may know that ye have eternal life."

Because of its unique content and the need of every believer it is recommended that you read this little five-chapter epistle every day for one week, making the appropriate notations in your daily diary. Try not to duplicate any that you have used, the book is so full of golden spiritual nuggets that won't be difficult. If doubts of your salvation persist after seven days, continue in 1st John seven more days, otherwise move on to reading priority number 2.

2. Read the Gospel of John twice. Like your first great need, the increase of your faith in general is vital to an effective Christian life. The best book in the Bible for that is the Gospel of John. The author does not leave us in doubt as to why he wrote the book, for in chapter 20, verses 30 and 31 he stated, "And many other signs truly did Jesus in the presence of his disciples, which are not written in this book; but these are written that ye might believe that Jesus is the Christ, the Son of God; and that believing ye might have life through his name."

It is said that the apostle John wrote this gospel around 85 A.D., long after the other disciples were dead. Matthew, Mark and Luke had been written some 20 to 25 years earlier giving a detailed record of our Lord's life, but John lived long enough to hear the teachings of heretics who began challenging the deity of Jesus Christ, suggesting that he was a great prophet, teacher or example, but denying He was the Son of God. The apostle, John, knowing he was the only remaining eye witness to the supernatural life of our Lord set out in the gospel that bears his name to include those events and teachings that leave no doubt as to the true identity of Jesus Christ. By the time you have read this book twice you will be in a good position to judge how well he accomplished his purpose.

You will find it profitable while reading John's gospel at the rate of approximately four chapters a day, in addition to your spiritual diary to make a list of the seven miracles John recorded that show Christ's supernaturalness. Many have found this book a vital aid to increase their faith. You should be able to read it twice in eleven days, that means in 18 days you will have read 1st John seven times and the gospel twice. (If you can't read that fast you should have this accomplished at least in 25 days.) That means that in less than one month your faith will be well grounded in the Word of God and you are ready to proceed to other books.

3. Read the Gospel of Mark twice. The Gospel of Mark compresses the life of Christ into 16 short chapters. It is an ideal book for busy people because he doesn't give a lot of details but covers a host of events in the life of the Savior in a short time. It is extremely important that you read and reread the gospels, for many times we are challenged to "let this mind be in you which was in Christ Jesus," or "as ye have received Christ Jesus the Lord, so walk ye in Him." How can we know the mind or walk of Christ unless we know His life? The only way to know that life is to read and reread about it in the gospels. If you are able to maintain the four chapters a day level we are suggesting, you can read this action packed gospel twice in just eight days.

4. Read the short epistles of Paul. Now you are ready for the nine short epistles of Paul: Galatians, Ephesians, Philippians, Colossians, 1 and 2 Thessalonians and 1 and 2 Timothy, Titus and Philemon. You will find these letters to churches or special Christian friends (Timothy, Titus and Philemon) to be delightful reading. If possible, try to read the entire epistle in one daily period; however, Galatians, Ephesians and Timothy will probably take longer. If you are using a Scofield Reference Bible, you would be wise to read the introductory material at the beginning of the book before you commence reading, otherwise, read about the book in *Halley's Bible Handbook*.

5. Read the Gospel of Luke. Now it will be profitable to return to another of the gospels of Christ, the book of Luke. This record of His life is the longest and most detailed; you will find things mentioned here that are not included elsewhere.

6. Read the book of Acts. After completing Luke's gospel, you will enjoy going right on with the story as he tells it in the book of the Acts of the Apostles. You will find it exciting to see how the Holy Spirit used the early Christians as they faithfully witnessed for Him throughout the then known world.

7. Read the book of Romans. The best doctrinal book in the New Testament is the book of Romans. Later in our course you should plan a study of the book, but now a single reading will afford you a bird's-eye view of the wealth of good teaching material found here. One reason this epistle is so unique is that it is probably the only one Paul wrote to a church he had never visited personally. For that reason it is thought to contain many of the concepts which he taught personally when founding a church. Don't be surprised if you find yourself rereading some sections several times. It will probably be difficult for you to read more than three chapters a day but try not to drop below that figure.

8. Read the entire New Testament twice.

It will take you eighty-seven days to read the New Testament through at the rate of three chapters a day. That means it will take you 174 days to read the New Testament through twice which is almost six months. The previous reading schedule will also take you about six months, meaning that in one year you will have read the entire New Testament through twice and the most important parts to young Christians several times. If you have never done this kind of consistent Bible reading before you will find it to be the greatest thing you can do for your spiritual life and maturity.

9. Read the wisdom literature of the Old Testament.

During this first year you have developed the consistent habit of reading the Word of God at least 15 minutes a day. In the process you have developed an overall picture of the New Testament and are now ready for key sections of the Old Testament. Incidentally, this first year has also made your attendance at a Bible teaching church more enjoyable and you are no doubt enjoying your pastor's sermons more because you have a better understanding of how what he is saying relates to the whole of the New Testament, that will increase as you proceed into the Old Testament.

The wisdom literature of the Old Testament contains most of the timeless principles of God that have been a stabilizing influence on the people of God for over 3000 years. The main books are: Job, Psalms, Proverbs, Ecclesiastes and the Song of Solomon. Rather than read them in that order, I would like to suggest a more helpful procedure.

First of all, begin this foray into the Old Testament wisdom literature by developing the habit of reading one chapter in the book of Proverbs daily. In my opinion, it is the most important book in the Old Testament except the book of Genesis, which explains man's origins. The reason I say that is because it contains more timeless principles to live by than any other in the Bible. Its author was endowed with two blessings, a devoted godly father who taught him the commandments, statutes and proverbs of the godly men before him plus Solomon was endowed by God with a unique gift of wisdom. In fact, the scripture says of him, "Before him there was none greater, neither would there be after him." "And God gave Solomon wisdom and very much understanding, and largeness of heart, even as the sand that is on the seashore. And Solomon's wisdom excelled the wisdom of all the children of the east country, and all the wisdom of Egypt. For he was wiser than all men,... and his fame was in all nations round about" (1 Kings 4:29-31). I believe the book of Proverbs contains the basic principles God wants man to obey to be happy and productive. He even promises that keeping them will lengthen your life (Proverbs 9:10, 11).

The book of Proverbs lends itself to daily reading by virtue of the fact that it has 31 chapters. If you start on the first day of the month you can develop the habit of reading the chapter that coincides with the calendar. By doubling up on the 30 day months you will stay in sequence. Many business men find this to be one of the most helpful things they have done to prepare them for the rigors of facing the daily pressures of the business world.

Since there are 212 chapters in Job, Psalms, Ecclesiastes and Song of Solomon, you will find that in less than four months by reading one Proverb daily and two chapters for the other wisdom books, you will read them through once and Proverbs four times. To fill in the remaining 32 chapters (because it actually takes 3 and one-half months), check the Psalms you enjoyed most as you read them and then go back and reread the 30 you liked best along with your Proverb each day.

10. Read selected books repeatedly. Once having digested the wisdom books, it is time to return to key New Testament books to read repeatedly as previously suggested. (Every day for thirty days.) This method of Bible reading is extremely beneficial in not only developing a rather thorough knowledge of that book, but it also helps its concepts to become a part of you. It may be that you will find other short books you wish to read repeatedly than those I suggest. After reading my reasons for selecting certain ones, if you feel yours are more beneficial for your needs, feel free to make the substitutions. Since there are eight months left in your second reading year, I make the following suggestions.

1st John. For the reasons already given, primarily for the bolstering of faith and the assurance of salvation. However, there are other valuable teachings in this five chapter epistle such as forgiveness, love of the brethren, testing spiritual teachers, guidance, prayer and much more.

Ephesians. The six chapters of Ephesians make it the longest in the group of suggested books, but it is exceedingly practical. It not only deals with the special blessings we receive in this church age, but it reveals the challenge to a spiritual walk in detail, shows the cure for anger, the most specific command in the Bible on being filled with the Holy Spirit, the most complete instructions on family living in the New Testament and sums it all up with a challenge to put on our spiritual armor so that we can stand against the devilish temptations of the adversary. Any Christian, no matter what his spiritual level of maturity, could profit from the reading of this great book every day for one month.

Philippians. The epistle of joy which Paul sent from a prison cell to the church of Philippi is a call to joyous Christian living. It lifts the spirit and more than any other book challenges us to a consistent walk above the circumstances of life rather than defeat below them. I have assigned the daily reading of this book to many sad and despondent Christians with quite remarkable success.

Colossians. This little epistle is a condensed version of several of Paul's writings, consequently, it is like drinking spiritual cream for the soul. You can find a new challenge every day for a month and still not exhaust its treasures.

1st Thessalonians. Paul was only in this city about three weeks yet he clearly taught them the Christian doctrine of resurrection from the dead and the second coming of Christ. In fact, he mentions the coming of the Lord in every chapter.

James. This five-chapter epistle is the balance wheel to the Christian life. It puts the life of faith in proper perspective by making it the motivation for faith. No Christian is prepared to serve God who is not familiar with the challenge to possess a faith that is demonstrated by works.

Romans 5-8. The heart of the teaching section of Romans is chapters 5-8, so try to read all four of these chapters each day for a month so you can get a basic understanding of them and their relationship to each other. In short, they cover justification by faith, the worthlessness of the flesh and our dependence on the Holy Spirit for victory in the Christian life.

John 14-17. As our Lord prepared to leave His disciples to carry on the work He had trained them for, He compressed some vital teachings they needed to know into the last few hours He had with them before His trial and crucifixion. These four chapters contain the gist of those important teachings. Every Christian should master them, for that reason they too are included in this schedule of repeated readings of important chapters and books.

If you follow this schedule carefully, you will have been reading your Bible daily with great profit for two full years. Now you are ready to...

Read the Bible through in one year. There are 1190 chapters in the Bible, 929 in the Old Testament, 261 in the New Testament. If you read three chapters a day and five on Sunday, you can read the entire Bible in 362 days. Many Christians read it through this way every year. One of the greatest Bible teachers I ever heard was the late Dr. Harry Ironsides who, at 72 years of age, had read the Bible through for each year of his life. Near the end of his life, he went blind, but kept right on preaching because he knew most of the Bible by heart.

Since there are only 216 chapters in the New Testament, it is suggested that you read one chapter from the New Testament each of six days of the week, then two from the Old Testament plus all five Sunday chapters from the Old Testament. Then on the 313th day of the year, you will have finished the New Testament and should concentrate on the Old until it is finished. Through this painless, but regular procedure, you will have in three years worked your way through the whole Bible once, the whole New Testament three times, the wisdom literature twice and many of the most important chapters and books several times. No matter how new a Christian you are when you start, if you keep up your spiritual diary as suggested, you will no longer be a baby Christian.

THE THREE YEAR BIBLE
READING SCHEDULE SUMMARIZED

First Year: Read ...
   1st John seven times
   John twice
   Mark twice
   Galatians through Philemon
   Luke
   Acts
   Romans
   The New Testament twice
Second Year: Read ...
   A Proverb every day for four months
   Two other wisdom literature chapters daily
   (Job, Psalms, Ecclesiastes, Song of Solomon)

Read repeatedly for one month the following:
  1st John
  Ephesians
  Philippians
  Colossians
  First Thessalonians
  James
  Romans 5-8
  John 14-17
Third year: Read ...
  One New Testament chapter daily
  Two Old Testament chapters daily
  Five Old Testament chapters each Sunday

6

The Bible Is The World's Greatest Library

The Bible is the most unique book ever written, for three reasons; one, it was written by a loving God to sinful man to instruct him in matters of both God and man. Two, it is not just one book, but a library of 66 books and three, it is the only book in the world that tells man the truth about the past, present and future. Consequently, it is not necessary to spend time proving its truth. You will, however, find it helpful to know something about how the Bible came into being and why.

The word "Bible" comes from the Greek word "Biblion" which means "book." When we think

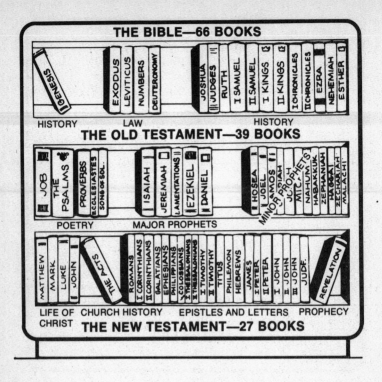

THE BIBLE—66 BOOKS

GENESIS EXODUS LEVITICUS NUMBERS DEUTERONOMY JOSHUA JUDGES RUTH I SAMUEL II SAMUEL I KINGS II KINGS I CHRONICLES II CHRONICLES EZRA NEHEMIAH ESTHER

HISTORY   LAW   HISTORY

THE OLD TESTAMENT—39 BOOKS

JOB THE PSALMS PROVERBS ECCLESIASTES SONG OF SOL. ISAIAH JEREMIAH LAMENTATIONS EZEKIEL DANIEL HOSEA JOEL AMOS OBADIAH JONAH MIC. NAHUM HABAKKUK ZEPHANIAH HAGGAI ZECHARIAH MALACHI

MINOR PROPHETS

POETRY   MAJOR PROPHETS

MATTHEW MARK LUKE JOHN THE ACTS ROMANS I CORINTHIANS II CORINTHIANS GALATIANS EPHESIANS PHILIPPIANS COLOSSIANS I THESSALONIANS II THESSALONIANS I TIMOTHY II TIMOTHY TITUS PHILEMON HEBREWS JAMES I PETER II PETER I JOHN II JOHN III JOHN JUDE REVELATION

LIFE OF CHRIST   CHURCH HISTORY   EPISTLES AND LETTERS   PROPHECY

THE NEW TESTAMENT—27 BOOKS

of a book we picture a hardback or well-bound paperback book that can stand upright on a shelf. Ancient books were written on papyrus reed and were made in the form of scrolls.

GOD'S THREE REVELATIONS

There are three specific ways God has revealed Himself to mankind.

60

1. Through Creation.

Psalm 19:1 says, "The heavens declare the glory of God; and the firmament showeth his handiwork." Romans 1:19-20 states, "Because that which may be known of God is manifest in them; for God hath shown it unto them. For the invisible things of him from the creation of the world are clearly seen, being understood by the things that are made, even his eternal power and Godhead, so that they are without excuse."

These and other scriptures clearly indicate that God has given ample evidence in creation that He exists. There are serious limitations to that form of revelation, however, for we do not learn a great deal about God's personal nature and nothing about His grace, love and mercy for man.

2. Through Jesus Christ

God has given a more specific revelation of Himself to man. Hebrews 1:1-3, "God, who at sundry times and in diverse manners spoke in time past unto the fathers by the prophets, hath in these last days spoken unto us by his Son, whom he hath appointed heir of all things, by whom also he made the worlds; who, being the brightness of his glory, and the express image of his person, and upholding all things by the word of his power, when he had by himself purged our sins, sat down on the right hand of the Majesty on high," Jesus Christ revealed God to man in everything He did; that's why if you want to know about God, then study the life of Christ. All man really needs to know about God is found in the person of the Lord Jesus Christ. But unless you happened to live during the time of His life, you would never have known about that revelation of God were it not for the Bible.

3. Through the Bible

Of the three revelations of God, the 66 books of the Bible provide us the most complete revelation information about Him and it is permanently in our grasp so we can study at our own discretion. He has prom-

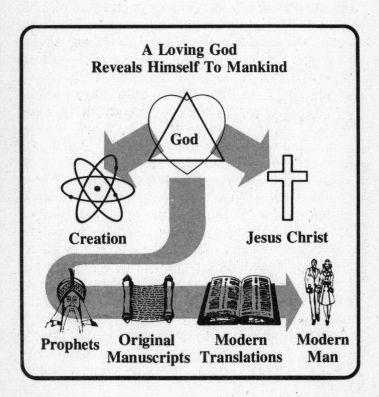

A Loving God Reveals Himself To Mankind

God

Creation

Jesus Christ

Prophets   Original Manuscripts   Modern Translations   Modern Man

ised to illuminate us through His spirit as we carefully read and study this third revelation. The diagram will describe the process and end result of God's revelation, the Bible.

THE ORGANIZATION OF THE BIBLE

One of the incredible things about the Bible is its amazing organization. No book of man could possibly have been written that way for it was not compiled by a single author within a particular life time, but was written by over 40 different people during a period of 1600 years, yet it shows the unmistakable hand of one overall mind. That can only be accounted for on the basis of God revealing Himself to these men during their various lifetimes. Most of them never knew the others and many were not aware that others were even writing. Yet when put together the sixty-six books in the library of God make one composite whole.

The reason for this unity and wholeness of design is not difficult to understand when you keep in mind that these men knew they were not speaking for themselves but God spoke through them. Consider the testimony of these writers:

Moses: "And God said unto Moses, I AM THAT I AM: and he said, Thus shalt thou say unto the children of Israel, I AM hath sent me unto you" (Exodus 3:14).

Joshua: "Now after the death of Moses, the servant of the Lord, it came to pass that the Lord spoke unto Joshua, the son of Nun, Moses' minister, saying" (Joshua 1:1).

Samuel: "And the Lord said to Samuel, Behold, I will do a thing in Israel, at which both the ears of everyone that heareth it shall

63

tingle" (1 Samuel 3:11).

David: "The Spirit of the Lord spoke by me, and his word was in my tongue" (2 Samuel 23:2).

Jeremiah: "The word of the Lord came also unto me, saying,... For thus saith the Lord, enter not into the house of mourning, neither go to lament nor bemoan them; for I have taken away my peace from this people, saith the Lord, even lovingkindness and mercies... For thus saith the Lord of hosts, the God of Israel, Behold, I will cause to cease out of this place in your eyes, and in your days, the voice of mirth, and the voice of gladness, the voice of the bridegroom and the voice of the bride... Therefore, behold, the days come, saith the Lord, that it shall no more be said, The Lord liveth, who brought up the children of Israel out of the land of Egypt" (Jeremiah 16:1, 5, 9 and 14).

The 39 books of the Old Testament were written in Hebrew by at least 32 different men, from a variety of educational and vocational backgrounds including priests, prophets, judges, kings, and shepherds covering a time period of approximately 1600 years. One of the first things you should do in the study of the Word is memorize the books of the Bible by divisions. This will help you find your way around in the Scriptures when discussing or hearing it taught and will better enable you to compare scripture with scripture.

The divisions of the Bible were not written in

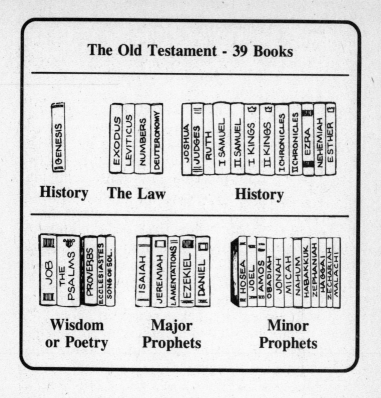

The Old Testament - 39 Books

History · The Law · History

Wisdom or Poetry · Major Prophets · Minor Prophets

this order but have been arranged in these groups for convenience sake. The Jews only have 22 books in their scriptures, for they combine such books as 1 and 2 Kings, Ezra, Nehemiah, Esther and others, but the content is essentially the same as our 39 books.

In the New Testament there is repeated reference to Moses and the prophets. This twofold grouping places the five books of Moses which we call "the law" division in one group and then lumps all the rest into another called "the prophets" because in a sense all the writers were prophets or spokesmen for God. You will find the five divisions make it much easier to remember how each book relates to the whole. The following descriptions will help you become acquainted with each division:

The Law

These books are sometimes called the "Pentateuch" or the five books of Moses, or the Jews call them "the Torah" meaning law. They consider them on a higher level of inspiration than the other O.T. books; we do not. The first six chapters of Genesis contain some of the most sublime literature in all the world dealing with creation, man's origin, the fall, and the conditions that led up to the world-wide flood. Obviously God did not reveal much to us about that period of about 1600 years from Adam to Noah, for it is all pressed into six chapters. This is in stark contrast to the other 923 chapters that cover a period of only about 2000 years in the history of Israel from Noah to Malachi. The stories of many men of God are recorded, including that of Abraham, Isaac, Jacob, Joseph, Moses and many others.

Included in these books are the history of man, the development of Israel as the "chosen people," their 40 years wandering in the wilderness and the giving of the law and God's special instructions to them as a people. These ancient books are among the oldest known to mankind and have teachings that are singularly unique. They defy human primitive concepts and standards but started out on such a sublime level they are still unsurpassed as literature, just as you would expect if they were really authored by God.

History

The next 12 books found in your Bible cover about eleven hundred years from the entering into the promised land under the leadership of Joshua to the partial restoration back into the land after the Babylonian captivity. You will find the exciting stories of judges like Gideon and Samson, kings like Saul, David, Solomon and many others. In a real way, it is the fulfilling of God's prophecy to Israel in Deuteronomy 28 that if they would obey Him He would bless them, but He warned that if they disobeyed Him He would curse them. As clearly seen in these books of history, the times of Israel's blessings followed their obedience to God, their periods of national disgrace and sorrow followed their times of disobedience.

One of the things you will enjoy is the characters God raised up at key periods of history. It reveals to us that He is indeed willing to use men and it also shows He is faithful to the individual that obeys Him. We are challenged in the New Testament to read these dealings of God with men because they are "examples" of how He wants to work in our lives today.

Wisdom or Poetry

We have already examined the importance of learning the wisdom literature of the Bible, so we shall not repeat it. But these timeless principles show how to enjoy success and blessing regardless the political and religious circumstances into which a person is born.

Some Bible teachers call these "the books of poetry" because they were largely written as poetry, particularly Psalms and Proverbs. That is why sometimes you will note that the writers say the same thing in the last half of a verse that they did in the first. This is called "Hebrew parallelism" and usually adds further insight into the original statement. Once you get used to it you will enjoy it. I have met many who read one Psalm and one chapter of Proverbs each day.

Care should be taken in reading the other three books. Job contains some bad advice that should not be taken as God's truth, but man's philosophical attempt to explain tragedy without God's insights. If you keep the overall story in view, you will have no problem.

Ecclesiastes is a different matter; it contains the frustrations of Solomon at the end of his life after turning his back on God and obedience to the principles of God that he well knew. Never build your life on the humanistic conclusions of this backslidden king, unless it is to recognize the futility of man apart from God.

The Song of Solomon contains the intimate story of the beauties of married love. It shows that God designed sex for married pleasure and love.

Major Prophets

The four prophets who wrote the five books called "major prophets" were the outstanding prophets in the entire history of Israel. Isaiah called the nation of Judah to repentance which saved the country from the judgment of God for another one hundred and thirty years. Jeremiah tried the same thing in his day but was rejected. His little book of Lamentations is his sad lament that the great city of Jerusalem and the nation of Judah were unnecessarily destroyed because they rejected the Lord. Ezekiel and Daniel were taken captive into Babylon and prophecied the restoration of Israel prior to the first coming of Christ and again in the "last days." Daniel's prophecy is considered outstanding in the Old Testament and is comparable to the book of Revelation of the New Testament.

Minor Prophets

The 12 minor prophets were raised up by God at strategic times in the history of Israel to call the people back to God. They are called "minor" prophets because their books are smaller. Although limited largely to the people to whom written, there are many blessings to be found hidden in these little prophecies.

THE SILENT YEARS

From the close of the Old Testament to the birth of Christ over 400 years transpired when Israel had no prophet to reveal the message of God. For that reason they are called "silent years." They were completed with the coming of the prophet John the Baptist.

The 27 books of the New Testament were written in Greek by eight men, three of whom (Matthew, John and Peter) were apostles who were eye witnesses of what they wrote except Luke who was a constant travelling companion of Paul, thus he saw many of the events he wrote about in Acts and researched those in the life of

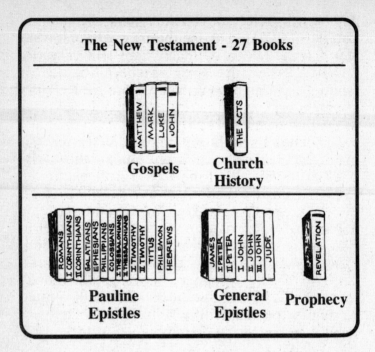

The New Testament - 27 Books

Gospels

MATTHEW · MARK · LUKE · JOHN

Church History

THE ACTS

Pauline Epistles

ROMANS · I CORINTHIANS · II CORINTHIANS · GALATIANS · EPHESIANS · PHILIPPIANS · COLOSSIANS · I THESSALONIANS · II THESSALONIANS · I TIMOTHY · II TIMOTHY · TITUS · PHILEMON · HEBREWS

General Epistles

JAMES · I PETER · II PETER · I JOHN · II JOHN · III JOHN · JUDE

Prophecy

REVELATION

Christ, in order to write the gospel that bears his name. Consequently, Luke is a presentation of the life of Christ as testified by the very people who saw the events recorded. The other gospel writers told what they had seen personally.

The first New Testament book written was James, about 50 A.D., the last one Revelation, was completed around 96 A.D., or approximately 46 years later. However, the events they describe covered a period of time close to 100 years, from the birth of Christ to John's vision of Revelation on the Isle of Patmos. Again, you are urged to memorize the names of these 27 books by their divisions so as to better familiarize yourself with the whole library of God.

The Gospels

The New Testament begins with the four histories of the life of Christ called the Gospels. Everything that can be known about the life of Jesus Christ is found in these four books; no other records of His life have been found. For that reason, it is of paramount importance that you read and reread them. No one of the Gospels is complete in itself. Some events of our Lord's life are included in all four, but each presents Him in a slightly different light, depending on to whom it was written or the purpose for its writing. To know His entire life you must familiarize yourself with all four of the Gospels. By reading 3 chapters a day you can read all four gospels in one month (that would be a good reading exercise for the first six months of your fourth reading year).

Church History

The 28 chapters of the book of Acts contains the only authentic record of the exciting spread of Christianity after the ascension of Christ. It is labeled the Acts of the Apostles, but it could well be called "the acts of the Holy Spirit," for His hand is vitally present throughout the book.

Written by Luke, a Greek medical doctor, it shows meticulous scholarship. So many geographical places are mentioned that several skeptics set out to disprove its authenticity by visiting them only to be overcome with its painstaking accuracy.

Pauline Epistles

The largest division of the New Testament is the thirteen Pauline Epistles. Each one was written to a church or person for some special purpose. Paul, "the apostle born out of due time," was the intrepid missionary of the early church who did more to spread Christianity than any man on record. His dramatic conversion is a classic illustration of the power of Christ to change lives, for he turned from being a Christ-hating Pharisee to a Christ-serving Christian. Almost every human need is covered in one or another of his epistles.

General Epistles

The general epistles are so designated because they were written individually for a specific need or to a group not reached by Paul. They cover a general area of truth needed by God's people of every age. Do not make the mistake of assuming that our lack of description of each book in this division indicates they are not important, for they are indeed literally filled with God's truth needed by today's Christians.

Prophecy

The last book in the library of God is very fittingly the greatest prophecy in the Bible, called Revelation. It is a revelation of our Lord during three stages of history: (1) The Church age; (2) The Coming Tribulation period culminating with the Second Coming of Christ; and (3) The New Order, which consists of the 1000 year Kingdom of Christ on this earth and the final replacement of this earth with a better and eternal one called "the new heavens and the new earth." This book is often considered the most exciting in the Bible, but admittedly is more difficult to understand than the others. Don't be surprised if there is much about it that you do not grasp by simple reading; this book has to be studied carefully in the light of many other passages of scripture. However, there is ample material in it that you can understand and from which you will receive spiritual inspiration to warrant your reading it frequently. (As an aid to understanding the more difficult sections, see the author's commentary on the book entitled, *Revelation–Illustrated and Made Plain*, published by Zondervan Publishing House.)

We have now briefly described the organization of the whole library of God as it appears today. You will find it a fascinating and inexhaustive library to study. It is the only book that is able to "make thee wise unto salvation..." (2 Timothy 3:15).

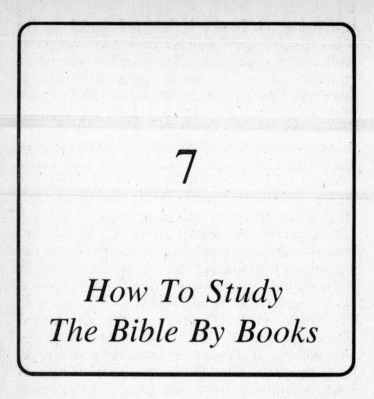

7

How To Study The Bible By Books

We have already seen that reading is the foundation of all Bible study. Next to reading comes writing, for both are an aid to memory and provide a handy source of reference and review in later days; that is why we advocate the developing of a personal Bible study notebook. The first section should contain your personal daily diary. After that should come the various methods of Bible studies that will be suggested in this chapter.

The simple devotional reading already discussed that is essential for daily spiritual growth is the easiest form of Bible study. I list it separately because it is, in my opinion, the very minimum spiritual food required to keep a Christian growing, but it is not enough to make him a strong *workman* for God. The theme verse of this book tells it very well, "Study to show thyself approved unto God, a workman that needeth not to be ashamed, rightly dividing the word of truth" (2 Timothy 2:15).

The key words in this verse are *approved* and *workman*. It is possible to be a Christian without any personal effort because salvation is a free gift of God. But if you are ever going to be an "approved workman" for God you will have to study the Bible. That shouldn't take you by surprise, for the same thing is true of anything today. To be a carpenter, plumber, plasterer or electrician you must study and serve as an apprentice for three to four years before becoming a journeyman or approved workman. Whether it is the construction field, or the professions all competent work takes study. You are no doubt well aware that as a general rule, the highest paid professions today, lawyers, doctors, architects and psychiatrists require the greatest amount of training and experience. The poorest paid jobs require the least preparation.

Recently I had the very sad experience of informing a forty-year old father of four that his job was being phased out and there was no other position in our organization that paid enough to support his family. What a waste! He was half way through life and totally untrained for any kind of work. As he left my office, I was reminded that the church is filled with many just like him, spiritually unprepared for any kind of Christian service simply because they are unskilled in the Word of God. Not only will this be reflected at the Judgment Seat of Christ when their bank account in heaven is examined, but it also keeps them from enjoying the maximum blessing in this life, which comes in serving Christ in whatever way He directs. The saddest part of it all is that it is entirely unnecessary; anyone with a real desire to serve God today can do so—if he is willing to study the Word of God.

Three things are required to successfully study the Word of God: mental work, discipline and time. If you put those three ingredients together, you can be a "workman approved unto God."

1. Mental Work. This book will help you in the "mental work" ingredient by making helpful suggestions on what to do and provide you with various charts to spark your thinking. This will keep you from floundering around in confusion and make it possible to get maximum training out of the time you have available for Bible study.

2. Discipline. You are the only person that can produce self-discipline in your life. It has long been my observation that discipline is the key to success in any field. That is why some young people who have graduated from Bible college fail in life. They never learned to discipline themselves while in school. They studied to pass tests and qualified for graduation, but had never been consistent in the daily study of the Word; consequently, they learned little or nothing of the Word after graduation. I suggest that you set a disciplined minimum requirement

76

on study just as you did for reading—otherwise, it will just become a good intention that never materializes.

3. Time. The minimum time allotment for study should be 15 minutes a day *in addition to reading!* For convenience sake this may be divided into three thirty minute segments a week or just lengthen your daily reading quiet time to 30 minutes with the last fifteen minutes being reserved for study. The only danger to this is that you might be tempted to run your reading time over into your study time and omit the study. For that reason it is best to have your devotional reading and Bible study scheduled at different times.

Many men and working women prefer to have their devotional time before going to work and reserve their Bible study for evenings. Housewives and mothers often prefer to wait until the family leaves for work and school and do both on a 30 minute period basis. Still others prefer to do their Bible study during their children's afternoon nap time. When you have it is really not so important. That you have it is!

One of the best illustrations of this was a 34-year old welder with an 8th grade education who I had the joy of leading to Christ. It turned out that his godly mother had been praying daily for his conversion for 27 years. When he was one month old in Christ he visited her and went to her little church. It just so happened that his sister was the Sunday School Superintendent and asked him to give his testimony which he did reluctantly. It took all of one minute and thirty seconds! I have never seen a man with a hunger to study the Word

77

of God like he had. It was largely for him that I worked out the study program in this chapter, which he followed consistently. Nine months later he visited his family again and his sister asked him to deliver a Bible study during the Sunday School hour, to which he gladly agreed. The entire congregation was amazed to see this 10 month old "babe in Christ" deliver a well thought out forty minute message. Afterward the young minister of the church asked him "what in the world have you been doing to learn the Bible that fast? I've never seen anyone grow like this before."

I watched that man go on to become an effective Bible teacher and soul-winner who has held almost every office in his church. The secret was mental work, plus self-discipline, plus time spent in the study of the Word. In his case it equalled rapid spiritual growth and usability as a "workman approved unto God." I'm sure it will in yours if you follow the same procedure.

PRIORITIES OF BIBLE STUDY

Just saying "study the Bible" can scare some people, for they don't know how to go about it. We shall consider seven of the best methods and I would like to list them in the order of their greatest importance; it is our suggestion that you follow in the order we list them, beginning primarily with number 2.

1. Study the Bible as a whole. We have already seen that the Bible is a library of 66 books, each written for a specific purpose yet with an over-all consistent message from God to man. It is important that you have an over-all picture of the whole Word of God so that

78

each of the other methods listed here can be studied in the light of the whole. You will find the over-all concept will naturally result from the three year reading program which we have outlined in the preceding chapter.

2. Study the Bible by books. The heart of a Bible study program is to study it as it was written, by individual books. As we have seen, each book was written to a church, group of people or individual. Most of them were written as letters and in all probability the author had no idea it was going to be a timeless message that would be studied by millions. God, of course, knew, and He was also aware that the basic problems, teachings and meanings would be just as relevant after two millenniums as they were in the day they were written.

CHOOSING
THE RIGHT BOOK TO STUDY

It is very important that you select the right book to study, particularly in the early days of your program for if you make a faulty selection you may get discouraged. The following suggestions should help in your selection.

1. Select a short book of no more than four to six chapters. It is obviously much more difficult to get an over-all picture of the 28 chapters of Acts or Matthew than the four chapters of Philippians or Colossians.

2. Select an easy book. Admittedly, some books of the Bible are easier to understand than others, for example, Revelation, 1 Peter, Hebrews and Romans are much more complex than 1 John, 1 Thessalonians, or the Gospel of John;

79

consequently, it is not advisable to start with them. Many of the questions that arise in these more difficult books will be more easily answered *after* you have studied some of the easier ones.

3. Select a book that is highly practical for today, one from which you can benefit spiritually as you study. Admittedly, all scripture is ... profitable but some is more profitable than others, particularly at different stages of your Christian life. The same list we suggested for reading would be a good guide to follow (see pages 57-58).

REPEATED READING

After selecting the right book to read, it is important to work on mastering the contents of the book. If you enjoy reading that is not really too difficult, all you have to do is read it repeatedly ten or twelve times in one sitting. That, of course, will take longer than we originally suggested, but you will be amazed if you will give three to four hours to doing this sometime just how much it will mean to you and how much you will get out of it. If you begin your study of a book after you have read and reread a book in your quiet time as previously suggested, you will find that extremely helpful also. Only after repeated readings will you begin to see the book "fall into place" in your mind, or see the various strains and fascinating lines of thought that run through it.

BASIC QUESTIONS TO ASK

Once you have read the book at least a dozen times, you are ready to begin answering some basic questions that will further help you to grasp the total book. The following list is prepared for that purpose:

1. Author?
2. What were the circumstances of the author when written?
3. To whom written?
4. Tell something about them.
5. Where written?
6. When written?
7. Why was it written?
8. What were the major problems?
9. What solutions were given?
10. What was the central meaning in that day?
11. What is the central meaning today?

Additional comments:

On the next page you will find a sample book study chart designed to fit into a medium sized notebook. Although it is copyrighted, you are at liberty to make copies for your own personal use (copies for resale are not permitted). Several additional copies are included in the last chapter, and if you so desire, printed pages in a pad of 25 may be purchased from Family Life Seminars. You will find this questionnaire a handy guide in this phase of your Bible study. When completed, it will provide an excellent source of review in the years to come.

OUTLINE THE BOOK

Once you have answered the above questions, you are ready to outline the book. To do so, you should have read it through sufficiently so that the main theme or purpose of the book stands out clearly. Reduce that to a single sentence and write it into the space provided on your Bible study outline form. Then select one or two verses that provide the key to the whole book and list them in the appropriate place.

As you prepare your outline, it would be wise to use scratch paper because you may decide to change it upon subsequent readings. Pick out the major topics, usually three to five points in the smaller books. Don't be deceived by the chapter divisions in your Bible. They were not done by the original authors, in fact, they didn't appear until the 14th century and they were done rather hurriedly, consequently some of them are located very poorly. You will find that sometimes two or three chapters cover a single subject, for example, 1 Corinthians chapters 12, 13 and 14 cover spiritual gifts.

After you are settled on the main divisions of your outline, then write them into the chart but leave room for sub points to be inserted later. It is best to cite the verses for each major and minor division in your outline.

Whenever possible try to coordinate your study of the Bible by books with the program previously mentioned of reading a book through every day for thirty days. Not only will you have read it over thirty times devotionally, you will have studied it until you have a working knowledge of that book so that with only occasional reviews of your notes, you should be able to remember most of its teaching for life.

Book Study

Name of Book _____ How Many Times Read? _____

Date _____

1. Author _____

2. What were the circumstances of the author when written? _____
_____
_____

3. To whom written? _____

4. Tell something about them _____
_____

5. Where written? _____

6. When written? _____

7. Why was it written? _____
_____

8. What were the major problems? _____
_____
_____
_____

9. What solutions were given? _____
_____
_____
_____

10. What was the central meaning in that day? _____
_____
_____
_____

11. What is the central meaning today? _____
_____
_____
_____

12. Additional comments: _____
_____
_____
_____

Book Study

Book _____ Date _____

Summarize the main theme: _____
_____
_____
_____

Pick a key verse: _____
_____
_____
_____

Outline _____
_____
_____
_____
_____
_____
_____
_____
_____
_____
_____
_____
_____
_____
_____
_____
_____
_____
_____
_____

8

Study The Bible By Chapters

Next to book studies, you will probably enjoy chapter analysis as much as any other kind of study. One advantage is that it is usually brief enough so that you can keep the central thoughts in mind. The most ideal division of any Bible study is the chapter. The reason for saying so is their length and content. The average chapter is about 25 verses, a handy length to read and although they often are divided into several paragraphs, they usually have one central lesson or subject. You will find them a handy length to work with and chapter analysis to be a rich source of blessing.

THE TWELVE CHAPTERS TO MASTER

All chapters of the Bible are not equally as rich as others to the believers of this age. However, there are hundreds from among the 1189 chapters that prove invaluable for study. The following twelve are, in my opinion, the most important for Christians to master and are listed in the order I consider them most significant (Group A). If you will analyze these twelve first, spending no more than one week on each, you will no doubt have found others by the time you finish from your daily reading which you will wish to analyze. In Group B you will find some of my additional suggestions in case you do not find your own.

Group A
Ephesians 5
Galatians 5
John 14-17
Romans 6, 8, 12
1 Timothy 2
Ephesians 4, 6

Group B
John 1, 3-5
Matthew 5-7, 13, 24-25
Matthew 26-28
John 11-12, 18-21
Acts 2-3
1 Corinthians 6, 15
2 Corinthians 4-6
Proverbs 3
Psalms 1, 27, 37

HOW TO ANALYZE A CHAPTER

All of the Bible is "profitable." Some passages, however, are more so than others. Like most any book, you should read some chapters once or twice, but others should be read frequently until they become a part of you. So it is with the Bible. Some chapters should be read so you can see where they fit into the whole library of God;

Chapter Analysis

Passage _____ *Date* _____

1. What is the main subject? _____
   _____
   _____
   _____

2. Who are the main people? _____
   _____
   _____

3. What does it say about Christ? _____
   _____
   _____
   _____

4. What is the key or main verse? _____
   _____
   _____

5. What is the central lesson? _____
   _____
   _____

6. What are the main promises? _____
   _____
   _____
   _____

7. What are the main commands? _____
   _____
   _____

8. What error should I avoid? _____
   _____
   _____

9. What example is here? _____
   _____
   _____

10. What do I need most in this chapter to apply to my life today? ___
    _____
    _____

Chapter Outline

Chapter _____ Date _____

Summarize the main subject: _____
_____
_____
_____
_____
_____
_____

Select the key verse: _____
_____
_____

Outline: _____
_____
_____
_____
_____
_____
_____
_____
_____
_____
_____
_____
_____
_____
_____
_____
_____
_____
_____
_____

others should be analyzed until they are mastered.

Analyzing a chapter is not difficult, but it does take time. Read the chapter through at least ten times. By that time you will begin to see the real purpose of the passage. The following questions will further aid you in understanding the chapter.

1. What is the main subject?
2. Who are the main people?
3. What does it say about Christ?
4. What is the key or main verse?
5. What is the central lesson?
6. What are the main promises?
7. What are the main commands?
8. What error should I avoid?
9. What example is here?
10. What do I need most in this chapter to apply to my life today?

You will find a handy notebook size chart on (preceeding) page to help make this chapter analysis. Additional charts will be found in the back of the book.

SUMMARIZE THE CHAPTER

Once the above ten questions are completed, you should proceed to make your own summary of the chapter. By this time you should know it so well that you can reduce the entire chapter to a three to five line paragraph. When that is completed, you are ready to make an outline of the chapter.

OUTLINE THE CHAPTER

Most good translations have simplified the process of outlining a chapter because they have separated them into paragraphs. The New

Scofield with the updated King James Version has a little paragraph symbol which is used to designate distinct changes of subject within a chapter. You will find paragraph analysis, that is, the detailed breaking down of a section into its main points, can be done to great profit.

Sometimes you will find that your chapter divisions are different than the publisher's. Remember, the Bible was not originally written with any punctuation or paragraphing, so your divisions are as good as anyone's. If you use the New Scofield, don't become enslaved to its paragraph or sub-paragraph headings. Many Bible students prefer the New American Standard Version, both for its modern phrasing, but also because, although it is divided into chapters, it does not have as many inserted titles. In either case, you should strive for originality. Outlining is quite simple once you have picked out the key paragraphs, they then become your main Roman numeral points. Once these are established, you can concentrate on the sub-points.

Within your paragraph there are two other smaller divisions that many students of scripture like to examine carefully. One is verse analysis. The Bible has many outstanding verses that are worthy of study and will provide great inspiration and spiritual blessing. Still another procedure is word studies, where you trace a word back to its original meaning by using a Greek or Hebrew dictionary (we shall describe how even those who have never taken Greek or Hebrew can do that profitably in another chapter), then find the first time the word is used, begin there and trace it through the scriptures. There are over 6,000 English words used in our modern Bible; obviously you will never run out of subject matter.

When your chapter analysis sheet has been carefully completed, place it in your notebook in a special chapter section. By rereading it for review from time to time, it will help the basic truth of this chapter to sink firmly into your mind. Years of classroom teaching has convinced me that review is essential to most memories. One of the dangers of an education is that once he has taken his final exam, a student is apt to forget most of what he learned. Periodic reviews will help considerably in the retention of the material you have learned. The mind is a marvelous conditioning mechanism—the best conditioning in the world is to "renew your mind" with the Word of God—that's why we have it!!

OTHER STUDY PROCEDURES

There are many other methods of Bible study.

Repeated Readings

We have already seen that reading is at the heart of all learning, and the best reading method is every day for fifteen to thirty minutes. The same thing applies for a single chapter except that you should read it over ten to twelve times before attempting an analysis. One thing you can do that will really make it come to life is underline the verbs. The action of a passage is shown in its verbs; consequently, after underlining them, you can easily see the flow of a passage by going back and studying the verbs. Consider the following passage in Romans 6:11-13:

Likewise, *reckon* ye also yourselves to be dead

indeed unto sin, but alive unto God through Jesus Christ, our Lord. *Let* not sin, therefore, *reign* in your mortal body, that ye should *obey* it in its lusts. Neither *yield* ye your members as instruments of unrighteousness unto sin, but *yield* yourselves unto God, as those that are alive from the dead, and your members as instruments of righteousness unto God.

Character Studies

Some of the most interesting people who ever lived walk through the Bible with a heavy foot. Someone has said there are approximately 2,930 different men and women in the Old and New Testaments. Admittedly, some are only referred to once or twice, but others were key figures in their chapter of history, like Adam, Abraham, Moses, David, Solomon, Daniel and hundreds more. The New Testament tells us their deeds were recorded for our profit and that "... these things happened unto them for examples (unto us) ..." (1 Corinthians 10:11). The examples aren't much good to us unless we take the time to study their lives. On the next page you will find a suggested character analysis form which will aid you in such a study. Additional forms are located in the back of the book.

Topic Studies

One of the ways we knew the Bible was authored by God, not just the men who wrote it, is its amazing consistency. That is clearly seen in the study of topics in scripture, for whether you are studying it in Genesis or Revelation you will always find a unity of thought. In fact, you do not really know God's mind on a subject until you

Bible Character Study

Character _____ Main Scripture Passage _____

Date _____

"These things happened unto them as examples unto us."

1. List other passages regarding his life. _____
   _____
   _____

2. Briefly describe his childhood, parents, family, education. _____
   _____
   _____
   _____
   _____

3. What character traits do you see in him—good and bad? _____
   _____
   _____
   _____
   _____

4. Describe his main encounter with God. _____
   _____
   _____
   _____

5. Who were his chief companions, were they a help or hindrance? _
   _____
   _____
   _____
   _____

6. How did he influence others? _____
   _____
   _____
   _____
   _____

7. What significant mistakes did he make? _____
   _____
   _____

(over)

8. Did he acknowledge and confess his sins? _____

_____

_____

9. What were his chief contributions in service to God? _____

_____

_____

_____

_____

10. Describe his family life. Was he a good parent? _____

_____

_____

_____

_____

11. How did his children turn out? _____

_____

_____

_____

_____

12. What is the primary lesson of his life that is profitable to you? ___

_____

_____

_____

_____

_____

_____

_____

_____

_____

_____

have examined every reference to that topic in the Bible.

Recently I did a study on "the will of God" that provides a good example. Christians frequently ask, "How can I find the will of God for my life?", for we all have to make many decisions as we go through life. The tragedy is very few have taken the time to discover what God has already written about His will. That can be done quite simply. Just look up in a concordance every reference to the will of God and write them on a sheet of paper. You will find that some are repeated one or more times. Group them, and read them over until they fall into a basic pattern. The following is what I discovered:

I. God has a will for your life! Psalms 32:8; Isaiah 58:11; Isaiah 30:21; Romans 12:1-2

II. Examples of God's will:
Christ—Luke 22:42, John 4:34
David—Acts 13:22; Acts 13:36

III. God's will for all men.
1. Repent and be saved. 1 Timothy 2:4; 2 Peter 3:9; Matthew 18:14; John 6:40.
2. That you be filled with the Spirit. Ephesians 5:17-21.
3. That you fill your mind with the Word of God. Colossians 1:9; Colossians 4:12.
4. That you surrender your will and body to Him. Romans 12:1-2.
5. Serve Christ with a willing heart. Ephesians 6:6-7.
6. Live a sanctified, morally pure life. 1 Thessalonians 4:3; 1 Peter 4:2.
7. Give thanks in everything. 1 Thessalonians 5:18.

IV. The reward for doing God's will. 1 John 2:17

V. The results of *not* doing God's will. Matthew 7:21.

Once you have learned the principles of the will of God as taught in His Word, you will find it very easy to know what to do. Ignorance destroys God's people and is the cause of much needless heartache. A simple topic study helps to avoid that, not only on the subject of the will of God, but a host of others. Would you like to know what God's Word teaches about fear, anger, sin, adultery, truth or any other subject? Do a topical study and discover it for yourself.

Prophecy Studies

One very interesting Bible study is prophecy, particularly in this day when it seems there are many things happening that appear to be fulfillments of Bible prophecies. It should be kept in mind that the main thrust in the scriptures is not just prophecy. Instead, they were written about God, the life of Christ, man, salvation and daily Christian living. Prophecy is dealt with only in passing; therefore, it occurs in several places throughout the Bible. In some books it only occupies a chapter or two; in others, it is just one paragraph within a chapter and in some cases it is only a single verse that contributes prophetic instruction. The following list of scriptures and their subjects is not intended to be exhaustive, but when studied will at least give the beginning student a basic knowledge of prophecy:

1. Matthew 24   The Olivet Discourse
   Mark 13

Luke 21	(This is the most important prophetic passage in the scriptures. It is a basic chronology of events to come given by our Lord.)
2. 1 Thessalonians 4:13-18	The Rapture of Believers
1 Corinthians 15:51-58	
3. 1 Corinthians 3:9-17	The Believer's Judgment (See also 2 Cor. 5:10; Rom. 14:10; 1 Cor. 4:5)
4. Ezekiel 37-39	Russian-Israeli Conflicts
5. 1 Thessalonians 2:1-12	The Tribulation Period (Read also Rev. 6-18)
6. Revelation 19:1-21	The Glorious Appearing of Christ (See also Rev. 17:14-18; Luke 17:22-37)
7. Revelation 20:1-10	The Millennial Kingdom of Christ (See also Isaiah 65:17-25)
8. Revelation 20:11-15	The Final Judgment of Lost Souls
9. Revelation 21-22	The New Heaven and Earth

Various descriptions of conditions in the last days just prior to and after the coming of Christ for the church:

2 Timothy 3:1-4:8—An acceleration of evil

2 Peter 3:1-18—Scoffers and willful man

Few studies you can make will motivate you to greater consecration and devotion to service for Christ than prophecy and the second coming of our Lord. "Beloved, now we are we the sons of God, and it doth not yet appear what we shall be: but we know that, when he shall appear, we shall be like him; for we shall see him as he is. And every man that hath this hope in him purifieth himself, even as he is pure" (1 John 3:2-3).

Christ Studies

Another inspiring topical study that should be suggested will be found in analyzing passages that particularly emphasize the deity of our Lord. Many verses throughout scripture give certain insights that together provide us a composite picture of Him. The following list is not complete, but will give you a base on which to start. Your own daily Bible reading will provide many others.

Isaiah 52:13 - 53:12	Christ's First Coming Forecast
Psalms 22:1-31	Christ's Crucifixion Forecast
Luke 1:1-80	Christ and John the Baptist's Births Forecast
Luke 2:1-52	Christ's Birth
Matthew 1:1 - 2:23	More on the Birth of Christ
John 1	Christ the Word
Matthew 3	The Baptism of Jesus
Matthew 4	The Temptation of Christ and Call of the Disciples
John 2	The First Miracle of Christ
John 5	Christ Heals a Crippled Man
John 6:1-14	The Feeding of the Five Thousand
John 6:15-21	Christ Walks on Water
John 9	Christ Heals a Man Born Blind

Jesus' Life and Teachings

Passage _____ Date _____

1. Is the passage: About His life or teaching? _____

2. Give the essential details of the events. _____
_____
_____
_____

3. Who were His friends? _____
_____

4. Who were His enemies? _____
_____

5. Why were they opposed to Him? _____
_____

6. What other passages tell the same story? _____
_____
_____

7. What other details do they include? _____
_____
_____

8. What do you learn about His deity in this passage? _____
_____
_____

9. Everything Jesus did expressed the nature and attitude of God. What did you learn about God in this passage? _____
_____
_____

10. What principles did He teach? _____
_____
_____
_____
_____

11. What can you apply to your life? _____
_____
_____
_____

Jesus' Parables

Name of Parable _____

Passage _____ *Date* _____

1. What circumstances led up to this teaching, if any? _____

_____

_____

2. Prepare a brief summary of the parable. _____

_____

_____

_____

3. List any additional details given in parallel passages. _____

_____

_____

_____

4. Does He give an interpretation? _____

_____

_____

5. What is the one central truth He is teaching? _____

_____

_____

_____

6. Is there something here for me to apply to my life? If so, how can I do it? _____

_____

_____

_____

_____

_____

John 10	Christ the Good Shepherd
John 11	The Raising of Lazarus
John 13	Jesus Washed His Disciples' Feet
John 18	The Mistrial of Jesus
John 19	The Crucifixion
John 20	The Resurrection
John 21-22	The Post-Resurrection Appearances of Christ
Acts 1	The Ascension of Christ
Revelation 1	The Vision of Christ by John
Revelation 2-3	Christ and the Churches
Philippians 2:1-16	The Self-Emptying of Christ
Colossians 1:9-23	The Glory and Present Work of Christ

By the time you have done a chapter analysis of each of the above passages, allowing about one week or one and one-half hours for each, you will have a thorough knowledge of His life and ministry. The chart on (preceeding) page will help you both in the study and in providing a handy review aid in the years to come. Some of our Lord's teachings were in parables, consequently we have a special chart just for them.

Psalm Study

The 150 Psalms of the Old Testament provide the Christian with a rich source of practical instruction and information. Some are very short (4-6 verses) and can be analyzed in a few minutes; some are very long (up to 176 verses) and can be broken down into several sections. A majority of the Psalms were written by King David, who in spite of the terrible sins committed at one point of his life, was really a dedicated man of God with unique insights. They provide some of the best loved passages in the Bible.

Originally, the Psalms were used as the hymn book of Israel. Many are written in Hebrew parallelism; that is, they say the same thing twice, but in a little different way. The second phrase or verse sometimes just repeats; other times it is an amplification of the first. Psalm 102:1 and 2 are good examples:

Phrase 1—"Hear my prayer, O Lord."

Verse 1

Phrase 2—"Let my cry come unto thee."

Essentially they say the same thing.

Phrase 1—"Hide not thy face from me in the day when I am in trouble."

Verse 2

Phrase 2—"Incline thine ear unto me; in the day when I call, answer me speedily."

Notice, in phrase two he adds two things to his petition—he wanted God to lean his ear to him and to do so *quickly*. Who can say he has never felt like that?

The word "blessed" occurs frequently throughout the Psalms. Basically that means "happy." For example, "Blessed is the man that ..." means "happy is the man...." You will find the Psalms to contain many practical keys to happiness. It has been my custom for years to prescribe the reading of the Psalms to all who are discouraged or joyless.

Almost all of the Psalms provide a rich Bible study, but the following have been particularly helpful to the author.

Psalm 1   The Introductory Psalm

Psalms Study

Passage _____ *Date* _____

1. To whom is this Psalm addressed? _____
_____

2. List the blessings and the conditions for receiving them _____
_____
_____
_____

3. What promises did you find? _____
_____
_____
_____

4. Are there any commands? _____
_____
_____

5. Is there anything that causes you to think particularly of Christ in this Psalm? _____
_____
_____
_____

6. What is the gist of the Psalm? _____
_____
_____
_____
_____

7. What central thought appeals to you? _____
_____
_____
_____
_____

8. What does this Psalm teach that you can do to be a happier or more blessed person? _____
_____
_____
_____

Psalms Study

Passage _____ Date _____

1. To whom is this Psalm addressed? _____
_____

2. List the blessings and the conditions for receiving them _____
_____
_____
_____

3. What promises did you find? _____
_____
_____
_____

4. Are there any commands? _____
_____
_____

5. Is there anything that causes you to think particularly of Christ in this Psalm? _____
_____
_____
_____

6. What is the gist of the Psalm? _____
_____
_____
_____
_____

7. What central thought appeals to you? _____
_____
_____
_____
_____

8. What does this Psalm teach that you can do to be a happier or more blessed person? _____
_____
_____
_____

	(Much heartache can be avoided by memorizing and obeying verses 1-3.)
Psalm 8	The Glory of God and His Messiah
Psalm 23	The Great Shepherd Psalm
Psalm 24	A Prophecy of Christ
Psalm 27	An Encouragement to Faith
Psalm 34	The Lord Takes Care of His Own
Psalm 37	The Faith-Rest Life
Psalm 51	A Cry for Forgiveness
Psalm 59	A Cry for Help
Psalm 66	Thanksgiving for all God's Blessing
Psalm 78	God's Dealing With Israel as an Example
Psalm 91	The Best Way to Live
Psalm 103	A Paean of Praise
Psalm 119	God's Description of the Scriptures
Psalm 127	The Blessings of a Family

The chart on the preceeding page will prove helpful in doing a study of the Psalms.

Proverbs Studies

One of my favorite studies through the years has been the book of Proverbs. It is the best book on principles to live by that has ever been written, and its timeless principles are as important today as they were in the day God delivered them to Solomon. Like the Psalms, all of them are worthy of study, but the following are sure to provide strategic blessing:

Proverbs 1	The Importance of Wisdom

The chart on the next page will prove helpful in doing a study of Proverbs.

Proverb Study

Proverb _____ *Date* _____

(The Proverbs were written to make man wise toward God and man.)

1. What is presented as wisdom? _____
_____
_____
_____

2. What negatives are condemned? _____
_____
_____
_____

3. What positives are commended? _____
_____
_____
_____

4. List the timeless principles. _____
_____
_____
_____
_____

5. Do you know other passages that say the same basic thought? ____
_____
_____
_____
_____

6. Is there anything you have been doing that is here condemned? ____
_____
_____
_____

7. Is there something taught here you need to incorporate into your daily life? _____
_____
_____
_____

Proverb Study

Proverb _____ *Date* _____

(The Proverbs were written to make man wise toward God and man.)

1. What is presented as wisdom? _____
_____
_____
_____

2. What negatives are condemned? _____
_____
_____
_____

3. What positives are commended? _____
_____
_____
_____

4. List the timeless principles. _____
_____
_____
_____
_____

5. Do you know other passages that say the same basic thought? ___
_____
_____
_____

6. Is there anything you have been doing that is here condemned? ___
_____
_____
_____

7. Is there something taught here you need to incorporate into your daily life? _____
_____
_____
_____

9

Tools For Bible Study

A craftsman will always have excellent tools. No workman will become a craftsman unless he has the right ones. The same is true of the Bible student. His tools are the Bible and good books about the Bible.

Most young Bible students tend to make one of two mistakes when it comes to Bible study aids. They either reject them altogether and study only the Bible, or they read so many books about the Bible they rarely read the Bible itself. Both approaches are wrong.

So far we have given many practical suggestions that will help the earnest young convert gain a good working knowledge of the Word of God in just three years. Now it is time to consider some invaluable tools or aids to Bible study.

TEN ESSENTIAL BOOKS

It is only natural that as a minister and author I am a lover of books. From the days when I devoured nineteen Zane Grey novels for a high school English Literature class until the present, I have been an avid reader. (I'm a great believer that you are what you read.) Consequently I have several thousand dollars worth of books in my study and home library. But *it isn't necessary* that you buy that many! In fact, I have developed a list of only ten books I consider essential for your library. You will find in these books all you basically need for your first three years of Bible studies. The following ten books, with a description of each, are listed in the order of their importance. In some cases, I include optional selections in the same category. You should not get two in one category until you have one in all ten. A good way to painlessly collect those books is to put them on your birthday or Christmas list.

1. A Good Bible. The first and foremost requirement for becoming a Bible student is a good Bible. The reader is probably well aware of the fact that there are all kinds of Bibles on the market from translations and paraphrases to mistranslations. How is a young Christian to know what is best? Since he is not a Greek or Hebrew scholar, he will have to take the word of those who are. Among those scholars of my acquaintance, the preferences are one or two Bibles today: (1) The New Scofield Reference Bible; and (2) The New American Standard Version. The Scofield Reference Bible is my first choice, not because I agree with all its footnotes, but for the following reasons. (1) It contains the best current revision of the King James Bible, which was translated by over 50 Bible scholars and has been edited through the years as a result of suggestions from many other scholars; consequently it is the most scholarly translation ever made. The main objection to the King James Version has been the 400 archaic words which have changed their meaning since the King James Version was translated. This has been corrected in the New Scofield because its 1967 edition updated those old words making it much easier to understand. This new edition retains the dignity of the old King James with a minimum of change yet enough to make it clear and easily read by anyone.

Many of my friends like the New American Standard Version because it discards the old English of the King James Version and they say it is a better translation of the Greek. Personally, I find it hard to read and rarely have been impressed that it casts new light on the Scofield edition.

(2) The paragraph headings are very helpful in marking distinct changes of thought and are excellent aids for review. It also is a help in finding a passage you have studied but have forgotten the reference. The major headings also contain the references for parallel passages.

(3) The footnotes are very handy and offer help to the new Bible student on the page where they are needed. Care should be taken, however, that

you realize these are man's suggestions and may not necessarily be right, although I have found them so much of the time.

(4) The marginal references indicate where you can find other passages that touch on the same subjects.

Taking all things into consideration, until the new Bible being prepared by Nelson & Sons is completed (scheduled for release in 1977 or 1978), it is this writer's opinion that the New Scofield Reference Bible with its updated King James Version is the best single Bible for the new student. It is both accurate and readable.

Other good Bibles the student should consider are the Thompson Chain Reference Bible and the Open Bible. Both use the Old King James translation.

2. Halley's Bible Handbook. One of the most helpful books ever written on the whole Bible for young Christians is *Halley's Bible Handbook*. Over 3 million copies in print tells the story of its popularity. It is recommended by more ministers, Bible teachers and Christian workers than any book of its kind. Its 860 pages provide the reader with more Biblical information that any other book its size. Although it is not a complete commentary, it does tell the reader something about every book in the Bible and gives a great deal of fascinating information about archeological findings that confirm Biblical accuracy, important information about the silent years between the testaments and much additional helpful material.

This book was not intended for scholars but is a very practical and readable book designed to in-

112

spire laymen to read and enjoy their Bible. Currently priced at $5.95, it is the best Bible study buy available today.

3. A Bible Concordance. An invaluable help in studying the Bible is a concordance containing all the verses in the scripture on a given subject. It provides the simplest method of determining what the full teaching of God is on that theme. For example, there is much confusion today among counselors on the subject of anger. Some justify it, others suggest it should be channeled into energy, some are afraid of repressing it, etc. Much of this confusion is eliminated when a study is made of the over 200 verses on anger in the scripture. When this is done, we find anger is a sin that grieves the Holy Spirit, causes murder, is contagious and should not dominate a Spirit-controlled Christian's life. Such a study of anger is really quite simple, for all the references in the Bible on that subject are found on one page in the concordance.

The best concordance on the market, in this writer's opinion, is *Strongs Exhaustive Concordance,* by James Strong, published by Abingdon Press. It is rather expensive and at 10 lbs. weight, is quite clumsy, but it contains the most complete listing of subjects and references available. In addition to including all the words in the Bible, it contains both a Hebrew and Greek dictionary with a handy method of looking up the original word. The proper pronunciation of each word in its original language is given along with the best meaning. This feature enables even those that are not language scholars to go to the root word and

113

check its accuracy. This is particularly important in a day when we have so many translations to choose from, many of which contradict each other. How is the layman supposed to know which is right? *Strongs Exhaustive Concordance* provides the answer.

4. A Bible Dictionary. Another handy tool that is a must for Bible study is a good Bible dictionary. Frequently you will find subjects, words, places or doctrines that need to be described fully. Where is a young convert to look for an accurate meaning? The same place he would look for anything—a dictionary or encyclopedia, except that those found in the average public library do not always include all Bible subjects. In addition, they are often written from a hostile or anti-Christian point of view. A Bible dictionary contains a thorough listing of all Bible subjects and was compiled or authored by someone specifically trained in the Bible, its customs, places and teachings.

The Bible dictionary I have enjoyed most is the 1192 page *Unger's Bible Dictionary,* by Merrill F. Unger, published by Moody Press. I have compared it with others in my library on many different topics and almost always find it superior to anything else in the field. If you wish something more exhaustive, the Zondervan Publishing Company has published a *Pictorial Bible Encyclopedia* by Merrill Tenny and others, in five volumes. Every Christian school library and ardent Bible scholars should have this set, but *Unger's* single volume *Bible Dictionary* is very adequate for the beginning Bible student.

114

5. A one volume Bible Commentary. Because of the antiquity of the Bible, its occasionally heavy theological subjects and the fact that it was written in a language and to a people quite different from our own, it is very helpful to have a trustworthy Bible commentary to turn to when a passage does not seem too clear. There are so many such commentaries available that it is difficult to select the best because personal opinion and usage enters into one's judgment and it is difficult to make an evaluation. It does seem to me that a young Bible student could easily get bogged down in an exhaustive commentary, plus the fact that multivolumed commentaries are quite expensive. For that reason I recommend a single volume commentary, for ease of use and expense.

Matthew Henry's Commentary, published by Zondervan Publishing Company, has been a favorite for many years. Somewhat wordy in its original five volume set, it has been edited down to one thick 2,000 page volume that contains the heart of his comments on the scriptures. Largely devotional in nature, it is popular among ministers and Bible students. Someone has said that Charles H. Spurgeon, one of the greatest preachers who ever lived, used it continuously. Although it has not helped me to preach like Spurgeon, I have used it for at least twenty-five years.

A more contemporary commentary has been published by Moody Press entitled *The Wycliffe Bible Commentary.* This 1500 page work provides scholarly comments and insights on every book in the Bible, and deals with almost every passage as it appears. Still another single volume commentary that is worth studying was compiled by Jameson Fausett & Brown.

6. The Bible Has The Answer. There are approximately 150 basic questions that come to people's minds as they study the Bible. Dr. Henry M. Morris, one of the world's finest scholars and Bible students, has compiled these questions and together with his friend, Dr. Martin Clark, has given some clear and helpful Bible answers. For example, "How do you know the Bible is true?" "How do we know God exists?" "How can one God be three persons?" "Was Jesus a revolutionary?" "Has modern science discredited the Bible?" "Was Jonah really swallowed by a whale?" and about 144 others. The authors selected some of life's most difficult questions and dealt with them Biblically and practically. Published by Creation Life Publishers of San Diego, you will find much help in this book.

7. Many Infallible Proofs. Although God commands man to accept Him by faith, He does not expect man to accept Him by blind faith. What is the difference? The Bible and the human mind. Man's mind will never come to faith on its own, but guided by the revelation of God and the Bible, he can logically believe in God. Dr. Henry M. Morris again has produced a superb book setting out clearly the logical reasons for accepting such subjects as "the virgin birth," "the nature of God," "the resurrection of Christ," "the inspiration of the Bible," "fulfillments of prophecy," "alleged contradictions in scripture," "scientific fallacies of evolution" and many others. Produced by Creation Life Publishers, this excellent volume should be read carefully by every Christian who would know the scriptures and why he believes them.

8. A Harmony of the Gospels. The beginning Bible student may find the events in the life of Christ as presented in one Gospel somewhat confusing when compared with that of another. Because each Gospel had a different author and was written to a different group of people or had a little different perspective, some of the events may at first examination appear to be contradictory. False teachers have seized on such seeming variations in the account to suggest the Bible is not reliable. In truth, there are no contradictions in the Bible, but many who were unlearned in the scriptures have experienced a spiritual setback at thinking there might be.

Johnston M. Cheney had such an experience. As a young man, his faith was so shaken he even questioned his salvation for a time. Fortunately he didn't stop studying the Word of God and gradually his faith and confidence in God's Word returned as he saw the answers to his questions emerge one by one as he scrutinized the passages in question. For twenty years he poured over the four Gospels until he almost had them memorized. When he had every seeming inconsistency adequately explained, he decided to write a careful Harmony of the Gospels to show how each event fits into the totality of our Lord's life. His excellent book, *The Life of Christ in Stereo,* published by Western Baptist Seminary Press, will help all who have questions in harmonizing the events of scripture.

Another excellent harmony I can recommend,

117

if it is still being printed, is *A Commentary and Harmony of the Gospels,* by Charles P. Roney, published by Eerdman's Publishing Company.

9. Bible Doctrine. The basic teachings of the Bible are often called "doctrines," meaning the special teachings that are unique to the scriptures. Since they are not taught consecutively (because the Bible was written historically, consequently the doctrinal teachings occur all through the scriptures) therefore all the passages bearing on a given subject have to be studied carefully to come to a complete understanding of the teaching. Such study requires years of training and research time the Christian layman seldom has available.

Fortunately, many great Bible scholars have written books explaining the most basic doctrinal concepts. Those every student should know regard the nature of God, and include special studies on the life and work of Christ, the Holy Spirit, the Bible, what's wrong with man, the future destiny of Christians, and a host of other subjects. My favorite book of Bible doctrines is called *What the Bible Teaches* by R. A. Torrey, published by Fleming H. Revell Company. Another good book on this subject in case you wish to study further is *Great Doctrines of the Bible* by Dr. William Evans, published by Moody Press.

10. The Supernaturalness of Christ. Jesus Christ is the heart of the Bible and the center of the Christian faith. If indeed He is the supernatural Son of God, we can accept everything He said as "gospel truth." The beginning student of scripture would be wise not only to "believe in Jesus Christ unto

118

salvation," but he should know the good logical reasons for his belief. Dr. Wilbur Smith, truly one of the greatest Bible scholars of the 20th Century, has written a masterful book called *The Supernaturalness of Christ*. You might find it heavy and philosophical in the first few chapters, but the book really picks up on the proofs of the bodily resurrection of our Lord. Before your three year study of the Word is concluded, you should read Dr. Smith's book.

No group of ministers will agree on the ten most important books for the beginning Bible student, but these have proven helpful to me through the years. I have recommended them to many others and am confident you will find them profitable—if you use them.

Most Bible bookstores carry these volumes, but if you are not able to secure a copy, you may write Family Life Seminars, 2100 Greenfield Drive, El Cajon, California 92021.

10

Hermeneutics

Hermeneutics is a careful method of Bible study that insures that the message God intended to communicate is accurately understood by man. The Bible is not a simple book, but a divine communication with humanity, using human authors to do the communicating. The reason a scientific method of study like hermeneutics is necessary is seen in the following diagram:

An infinite God who is a spirit knows everything about everything. In trying to communicate to man, His creature who has only a limited amount of intuitive knowledge, He must use his

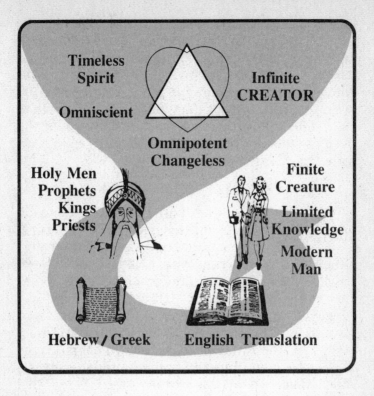

Timeless Spirit

Omniscient

Infinite CREATOR

Omnipotent Changeless

Holy Men Prophets Kings Priests

Finite Creature

Limited Knowledge

Modern Man

Hebrew / Greek

English Translation

eyes and ears, for that is the way man learns most things. The problem is further complicated because man speaks various languages; therefore, God must express His infinite concepts in one basic language and have it translated into the other various languages of mankind. Again, the communication process is complicated in that words, idioms and customs have changed during the over thirty-five hundred years since He first began revealing His mind and will to man in a written record. Therefore, there must be some accurate system devised to guarantee that what God said and meant so long ago is what present translations say and mean to modern man. That accurate system is known as hermeneutics. It is a logical, scholarly and trustworthy attempt to accurately assure that modern man understands the message God originally set out to communicate to him. The following hermeneutic rules guide the careful students of all generations to "rightly divide the Word of Truth."

HERMENEUTIC RULES

1. Take the Bible Literally. Much harm has been done by trying to spiritualize the Bible instead of taking it literally. When a person writes you a letter you do not spiritualize its meaning, but you take it literally to heart. The same is true of the Bible. There are, however, some few passages in the scriptures that should be taken spiritually. The question is, "How is the student to know which passages should be taken literally and which ones spiritually?" The best answer I know is the Golden Rule of Interpretation designed by the late Bible scholar, Dr. David L. Cooper:

"When the plain sense of scripture makes common sense, seek no other sense, but take every word at its primary literal meaning unless the facts of the immediate context clearly indicate otherwise."

You'll rarely go wrong in Bible study if you first try to interpret a passage literally. For example, when the Bible says "fire and brimstone fell out of heaven," it literally means fire and brimstone came down on the earth. When, however, the Bible says the moon turned to blood or the

Nile River turned to blood, as it did in the days of Moses, it does not mean literally it turned to blood, but it turned to a blood-like color. However, even in the case of the Nile River, it resulted in the death of fish. A good rule to follow is try to interpret it literally. If this is obviously not the case, then as a last resort try the spiritual interpretation.

2. Keep it in Context. It is always good to use scripture verses to prove a teaching or principle, but it is important not to lift a verse out of its context; otherwise, as we have previously seen, instead of it being a prooftext, it becomes a pretext.

3. Watch for Idioms. Every language has its idioms. In fact, idioms are one of the most complex parts of language study. For example, have you ever thought about the difficulty encountered by foreigners in learning English when they come upon such common idioms as "saved by the skin of your teeth." One of the things that complicates the use of idioms is that they change their meaning from one generation to another. For example, my teenage children were quite put out with me one time when I asked their group, "How are you making out?" only to find that the term "making out" had changed its meaning since I was their age. Usually a good Bible commentary will point out the idiomatic use of language and explain the meaning in the day in which it was written.

4. Be Alert to the Figurative Use of Language. When language is not used literally, the author will often resort to figures of speech. We're used to that in English, and you are probably familiar with the five most common—metaphors, similes, analogy, hyperbole and personification. We shall examine each of these briefly.

(1) Metaphors. A metaphor compares two things by identifying one with the other. Usually one of the metaphors is easily recognized and is used to clarify the other that is not so easily understood. It is the way we communicate from the known to the unknown. For example, in Matthew 5:13 it states, "Ye are the salt of the earth," meaning just as salt is a flavoring influence in food, so Christians should be a flavoring influence morally in their society.

It is the use of metaphors that has given rise to spiritualizing scripture because most metaphors are symbols. The most important in all the scripture is one found in Luke 22:19-20, where Jesus took bread and said, "This is my body which is given for you." The bread was bread; it was not His body. Obviously, it was a symbol of His body. The same is said of the cup, when He said, "This cup is the new covenant in my blood." We do not drink the blood of Christ when we partake of the grape juice; instead, we drink grape juice which symbolizes His blood. To the careful reader trying to literalize the scripture, the use of metaphors is not really a problem because they are usually quite obvious.

(2) Similes. A simile compares two things and usually the words "like" or "so" or "as" are used to introduce them. For example, our Lord said in Matthew 10:16, "Behold I send you forth as sheep in the midst of wolves." The obvious simile is in comparing Christians to sheep and

false teachers to wolves. This is a basic simile that is used in many places in the scripture. Again, it is not difficult to recognize them.

(3) Analogy. An analogy is a comparison of two things wherein one explains the other. Usually, an analogy is used as a type of reasoning. For example, in 1 Corinthians 1:18, Paul said, "For the preaching of the cross is to them that perish foolishness, but unto us which are saved it is the power of God."

(4) Hyperbole. A hyperbole is a deliberate attempt to exaggerate for the purpose of attracting attention. For example, in Matthew 7:3, our Lord said, "And why beholdest the mote that is in thy brother's eye but considers not the beam that is in thine own eye?" Obviously, no man could have a beam in his eye, but that hyperbole calls attention through exaggeration to the tragic result of criticism.

(5) Anthropomorphism. This big word essentially means ascribing human characteristics to God. The Bible teaches that God is a spirit and consequently does not have a body. But it is impossible for man to understand a spirit. Therefore, it was essential for God to use human body characteristics to describe Himself; thus we find the Lord's "ear" or the Lord's "voice" or the Lord's "hand." God hears us and He speaks to man and He sustains man, but He does not have eyes or hands or ears as we do. But in His own divine way He accomplishes the same. Therefore He uses the finite characteristics of man which man can easily understand to describe His infinite characteristics which otherwise man could not understand. It is wrong, however, to infer as some

have, that God has literal ears and hands like man.

5. Treat Parables Differently. A parable is an earthly story with a heavenly meaning. The best way to describe the need for parabolic teaching is to suggest that you envision yourself as a missionary to a tribe of Indians who have never seen electricity, refrigeration or any modern inventions. How would you describe to such the appliances in your kitchen? You would have to painstakingly use something within their frame of reference to use as a picture or parable to convey your meaning. The same is true in communicating heavenly or divine truth. Jesus Christ was a master at using parables. Oftentimes these parables are introduced by the statement, ''The kingdom of Heaven is like...'' or ''A certain man went into a far country...''

When it comes to interpreting them, most people overwork parables, that is, they try to make every single detail mean something special. In so doing, they often destroy the basic meaning. A parable is an illustration, and just as when you give an illustration of something you are trying to communicate it has one central truth, so does God's. But almost every illustration can be distorted and twisted way out of proportion by trying to apply every segment of it to something specific. For that reason you should be content to find that one central meaning of a parable and accept it.

These five simple rules are not all the rules of hermeneutics, but they are the ones that you should familiarize yourself with because they are the ones you are most likely to confront. You will find their literal application to Bible study will produce an accurate interpretation of God's message.

11

Accelerating The Learning Process

"Blessed is the man who walketh not in the counsel of the ungodly, nor standeth in the way of sinners, nor sitteth in the seat of the scornful.

"But his delight is in the law of the Lord; and in his law doth he meditate day and night.

"And he shall be like a tree planted by the rivers of water, that bringeth forth its fruit in its season; its leaf also shall not wither; and whatsoever he doeth shall prosper" (Psalm 1:1-3).

"Wherewithal shall a young man cleanse his way? By taking heed thereto according to thy word."

"Thy word have I hidden in mine heart, that I might not sin against thee" (Psalm 119:9, 11).

Scientists tell us there are 12 billion brain cells in the average human mind, but most people only use 10% of their brain's potential. Before the use of note pads and handy writing materials, people developed the habit of remembering much of what they heard; it was the only way they had of recalling things from the past which they needed.

In recent years, there has been a revival of this lost art of memorizing and I have observed that those who use it to learn scripture grow rapidly in their spiritual lives. Dawson Trotman, founder of the Navigators, probably inspired more people to memorize the Word of God than anyone in the 20th century. He said, "Nothing pays greater dividends for the time invested than writing God's Word on the tables of the heart." I have seen many individuals take spiritual giant steps as soon as they started memorizing scripture.

YOU CAN MEMORIZE!

When it comes to memorizing, most people confess to a "mental block." Only in rare instances is that really true. Most of the time the problem is an ambition block. If I were to ask for your address or phone number, you would have no trouble recalling it. Anyone that can do that can memorize Bible verses. Very honestly, memorization involves hard work but it pays greater dividends to your spiritual life than any other known method of Bible study.

128

WHAT MEMORIZING SCRIPTURE
WILL DO FOR YOU

1. It will give you victory over sin. "Thy word have I hid in my heart that I might not sin against thee" (Psalm 119:11). Nothing puts the brakes on a temptation to sin like the Word of God tucked away in the mind. Many a defeated, sin enslaved Christian has turned into a spiritual giant by learning the Word of God. Most of the sins that "so easily beset us" don't really overpower us, they just ease us over the line between temptation and obedience. The red lights of the Word of God flashing in our mind when temptation rears its ugly head is often enough to stop us in our tracks. Each time you heed the Word and reject the inclination to sin, you strengthen your spiritual life and make it easier to refuse the next time. Victory over sin is a gradual process and memorizing the Word speeds up that process.

2. Helps you overcome worry. Worry, anxiety and fear are as natural to a human being as building dams are to beavers. That's why the Word of God has so much to say about "fear not," "let not your heart be troubled," and "take no anxious thought for tomorrow." But such injunctions are of little value if you don't have them cemented in your mind when you need them.

Many times as a college president, pastor, or founder of Family Life Seminars and founder of a kindergarten through high school Christian school system, I have been tempted to panic in the face of budgets totalling almost 5 million dollars annually. When I look at the economy, the many family heads who depend on these ministries for their livelihood, it is tempting to "panic," particularly in times of recession or inflation. On such occasions my treasure house of memorized scripture brings welcome relief by flooding my mind with the principles of God. Mentally saying, "What in the world are we going to do" does nothing for me. But rehearsing in my mind the promise "my God shall supply *all* your need according to His riches in glory by Christ Jesus" certainly does!

3. It will give you confidence in sharing your faith. Once you become a Christian, you have a natural desire to see others come to Christ. But cold, naked fear is the most common deterrent to witnessing there is. The greatest fear most Christians have is that they either don't know what to say or they will say the wrong thing. That can almost never happen if you have made a habit of memorizing key verses. You don't have to be a super extrovert or a great debater to be a good witness for Christ. But you must know some of the key witnessing verses to be effective.

The first time I really saw the power of the Word in the mind of a Christian was in hearing the testimony of a former submarine sailor named Rosenberger. This convert from Judaism told how he rejected everything supernatural and blatantly ridiculed Christians. A brand new convert was assigned a bunk next to his and Rosenberger caught him memorizing his "3 verses a week," as taught by his Navigator buddies just before his ship sailed for the Pacific. The lad didn't know any

Christian arguments with which to answer Rosenberger's taunts and sarcastic barbs; all he knew was Bible verses, so each time he answered with "the Bible says..." and quoted him a verse. Ten months of that was all Rosenberger could stand before bowing to the forgiving grace of God. The Heavenly Father says of His Word, "my Word ... shall not return unto me void, but it shall accomplish that which I please..." (Isaiah 55:11). He makes no such promise for our words.

A Christian going out to witness without arming himself with the Word of God is like a soldier going into battle without a gun.

4. It Speeds Up The Transforming Process. All Christians are challenged to be "transformed" that is, walk like "new creatures" (2 Corinthians 5:17). That doesn't happen overnight—it is the result of a long process of growth. Memorizing scripture, however, will speed up the process remarkably because the secret to transformation is "renewing your mind" (Romans 12:2) through the Word of God. The more scripture you learn and incorporate in your life, the faster you will conform your life to the wisdom of God as the Bible teaches.

This renewing of the mind by memorizing the Word is particularly effective in changing your thought life. Most men have to fight mentally to keep themselves from lustful thoughts and evil imaginations. Memorizing scripture gives them something positive to think about rather than just guarding against harmful thoughts. This same technique has proven helpful to those who have to guard their thoughts against envy, resentment, revenge or other thought patterns that are contrary to God's will for your mind.

5. It Assists You Discover God's Will for You. Sometimes you have to make instant decisions in life and there is no time to run to your Bible or notebook studies. With a backlog of scripture stored in the cells of your brain, you will find it much easier to make the right decisions.

6. It Helps in Your Other Bible Studies. The best commentary on the Bible is the Bible itself. The more basic verses you have in your mind the easier it is for you to understand scripture in the light of other scripture. Young Christians often spend a lot of time reading commentaries about the Bible. But after you learn scripture you will find that commentaries will take less of your time and may only be used when confronting a difficult passage or in preparation for a public message.

7. It Outfits You for Unlimited Service to God. Through the years I have noticed that many college graduates end up in a profession quite unrelated to either their major or minor course of study. The reason for that is that colleges, particularly a Christian college curriculum, provide a broad base from which to launch a professional career. The door of opportunity usually opens to a person who is successfully occupied. The education gives him the background upon which to draw that enables him to be professionally flexible. Memorizing scripture does the same for a Christian. There is almost no limit to the potential of the child of God with a good mental grasp on the Bible.

132

HOW TO EFFECTIVELY
MEMORIZE THE SCRIPTURE

The best way I know for memorizing the Word is to use scripture memory cards. Some use 3 × 5 cards, some use calling card-size, but the important thing is that you carry your current memory cards with you wherever you go. That way you can review your verses during handy moments throughout the day—waiting in the dentist's office, at the bus stop, as you drive to work or whenever you have a spare moment to "redeem the time." The following suggestions will help simplify your memorization.

1. Write the Verse on Cards. Copying the verse right from the scripture on to a card in your own handwriting is helpful in starting the memorizing process. Having them typed up looks better, but it doesn't do as much for your mind initially.

2. Learn the Verse by Topics. Just learning verses and their references can be rather confusing unless you take a few seconds longer to learn a subject or topic for each verse. Rather than learn 50 random verses, it is far more effective to learn one verse for fifty different subjects. The reason for that is that the mind functions by subjects. When you want a verse on prayer or some other subject, it is simple to think of one if you assigned that topic to the verse when you learned it. The examples on the following page will illustrate the point.

Several experts in this field suggest it is best to learn three verses for each basic Bible subject before going to the next topic. There are two reasons for that. It is easier to remember them in groups of three if you originally learned them that way, rather than when you learn one each for fifty subjects. Another reason is because as a young Christian, some subjects are more important for you to memorize at first than others. At the end of this chapter is a list of three verses for fifty different subjects that should be learned in your program for gaining a working knowledge of the Bible in three years.

3. Learn the References. Always learn the references while memorizing the verse otherwise you will end up in confusion with a lot of scriptures in your mind but no idea where they are located. Someone has compared it to learning to associate names with faces. You can get by without remembering names, but you will find it much better if you learn to call people by their right name. In fact, the little extra time it takes to learn the references has been reported to also sharpen one's memory for names.

4. Memorize Three Verses a Week. Three verses a week is a time-proven ideal for scripture memory. More than that tends to be confusing to recall over a period of time and less than that often fails to keep you interested in scripture memory. At one period of my memory program, I got eager and accelerated to six verses a week. To this day, the hardest verses for me to recall accurately are the ones I learned at that time. Three verses a week give you ample time to learn them thoroughly with excellent recall.

5. Date and Record Each Verse. It is a good policy to put the date you begin learning a new verse on the back of the card. You should also keep a record in your Bible study notebook in case you ever lose your pack of verses.

6. Read the Verse Aloud and "Picture" it in Your Mind. The easiest way to memorize a new verse, after writing it down on your card with its subject and reference, is to read it aloud ten times, photographing it carefully as you read. After the tenth time close your eyes and mentally "picture" the entire verse. Say it aloud from memory, only looking at the card when necessary. After you have said it successfully several times without resorting to the card, you are ready to go on to the next verse. The ideal policy, if you have enough time, is to learn your three verses the first day of each week. This way when you can say all three of them without help, you are reasonably sure that by reviewing them three or four times a day, you can retain them easily by the once a day review method to be explained. Memorizing three new verses can usually be done in thirty minutes, the rest of your review program can ordinarily be done in your spare time, as long as you carry your "current" verses with you.

7. Review Daily. Educators tell us that "review is an aid to learning." It is imperative that you review your current week's verses several times a day, particularly at the first of the week. Once you have said a new verse three times perfectly, put it in your once a day group. But the first time you miss a word, bring it forward to your "current" section to be reviewed seven times a day.

8. 7 Week Daily Review. The secret of lasting memorization is to review each verse *daily* for seven weeks. It has been discovered that if you do, then you can remove those verses to a once a week program for seven months, after which you can drop them into a once a month review. Someone has said, "Review a verse daily for seven weeks, once a week for seven months, then once a month for seven months and you will remember it for life." I have found that I have to review verses once a month indefinitely or they may cause some trouble in recall.

136

A handy way to arrange your verses for review is as follows:

    I. Current Daily Pack—Not more than 21 verses divided into two groups (rubber bands make good dividers).

        1) 3 current verses and those missed during last review—review three to four times daily.

        2) 18 verses you review once daily.

    II. Once a Week Pack—after the eighteenth week of your program, you should add three new verses a week to this group for seven months.

   III. Once a Month Pack—It will take about nine months to start putting verses into this group, but by the time you do, you will be convinced of the worth of this program of scripture memory.

TOPICS AND VERSES TO LEARN

A. The following verses are the minimum every new Christian should know.

> *Topic*
> The Word—Commanded to Learn
> Assurance of Salvation
> Obedience—The Key to Happiness
> The New Life in Christ
> Witnessing—Commanded
> Daily Prayer is essential

B. This next set of verses will help you to intelligently share your faith.

> God Loves all Men
> All Men are Sinful
> The Results of Sin
> Christ Paid for Man's Sin
> Salvation is a Free Gift
> Christ is the Only Way of Salvation
> Man Must Receive Christ Personally
> Man Must Make Christ Lord of His Life

C. This section shows the results of becoming a Christian.

> Pardon from Sin
> Peace with God
> A New Nature
> New Power Within
> Victory Over Sin
> Victory Over Worry
> Victory Over Anger
> Victory Over Depression
> The Holy Spirit

138

Set I	Set II	Set III
Josh. 1:8	Matt. 4:4	Col. 3:17
1 Jn. 5:11-12	Jn. 5:24	Rom. 8:1
Jn. 13:17	Luke 11:28	Ps. 119:1-2
2 Cor. 5:17	Jn. 10:10b	Col. 2:6
Acts 1:8	1 Pet. 3:15	2 Tim. 4:2
Jn. 15:7	Jn. 16:24	1 Thess. 5:17

Jn. 3:16	1 Jn. 3:16	Rom. 5:8
Rom. 3:23	Jn. 3:19	Rom. 3:12
Rom. 6:23	Heb. 9:27	Rom. 5:12
1 Cor. 15:3-4	1 Pet. 3:18	Gal. 3:13
Eph. 2:8-9	Rom. 3:24	Titus 3:5
Jn. 14:6	Jn. 10:9	Isa. 53:6
Jn. 1:12	Rev. 3:20	Jn. 5:24
Rom. 10:13	Rom. 10:9-10	Acts 16:31

1 Jn. 1:9	Eph. 1:7	1 Jn. 2:1-2
Jn. 14:27	Jn. 16:33	Isa. 26:3
1 Pet. 1:23	Eph. 4:24	2 Pet. 1:4
Col. 1:11	Eph. 3:20	Zech. 4:6
1 Cor. 10:13	1 Jn. 5:4-5	2 Cor. 2:4
Phil. 4:6-7	2 Tim. 1:7	1 Pet. 5:7
Eph. 4:30-32	Ps. 37:8	Ecc. 7:9
1 Thess. 5:18	Col. 1:12	Ps. 100:4
Rom. 8:14	Jn. 14:26	1 Cor. 2:12

D. This group shows the new challenge that faces you as a Christian.

> *Topic*
> To Separate from the World
> To Follow Christ
> To Go and Witness
> To Grow in Faith
> To Walk in the Spirit
> To Be Generous
> To Yield Yourself to God
> To War a Good Warfare
> To Seek Christian Companions

E. These verses show what new characteristics you can expect to find in your life.

> Love
> Joy
> Faith
> Humility
> Patience
> Wisdom
> Grace
> Comfort
> Forgiveness

F. These verses include essential teachings you should know about certain subjects.

> God
> Jesus Christ
> Christ's Resurrection
> The Word of God
> The Second Coming
> God Rewards Faithful Service
> The Will of God
> Good Works
> Heaven
> Man's Ways Not God's Ways

Set I	Set II	Set III
1 Jn. 2:15-16	2 Cor. 6:17-18	Rom. 12:2
Luke 9:23	1 Jn. 2:6	1 Pet. 2:21
Matt. 28:19-20	Acts 1:8	1 Pet. 3:15
Heb. 11:6	Rom. 4:20-21	Acts 27:25
Gal. 5:16	Eph. 5:18	Col. 3:16-17
Luke 6:38	2 Cor. 9:7	1 Cor. 16:2
Rom. 12:1-2	Rom. 6:13	Rom. 6:16
Eph. 6:10-11	2 Tim. 2:3-4	Eph. 6:13
1 Cor. 15:33	Prov. 4:14	Ps. 1:1

Jn. 15:12	Jn. 13:35	1 Thess. 3:12
Jer. 15:16	Jn. 15:11	1 Pet.1:8
Eph. 6:16	James 1:6	Rom. 5:1
Rom. 12:3	1 Pet. 5:5	James 4:10
Heb. 10:36	Rom. 12:12	James 1:4
Matt. 7:24	2 Tim. 3:15	James 3:17
1 Cor. 1:4	1 Pet. 4:10	1 Cor. 15:10
2 Cor. 1:3-4	Jn. 14:18	Jn. 14:1
Matt. 6:14	Mark 11:25	Luke 17:4

Ps. 14:1	Prov. 1:7	Rom. 1:20
Phil. 2:9-10	Col. 1:15-16	Heb. 1:1-3
1 Thess. 4:14	1 Pet. 1:3	Eph. 1:20
2 Tim. 3:16-17	Heb. 4:12	2 Pet. 1:21
Jn. 14:2-3	1 Thess. 4:16-17	Titus 2:12-13
2 Cor. 5:10	1 Cor. 3:13	Rom. 14:10
Matt. 12:50	Jn. 7:17	Eph. 6:6
Eph. 2:10	Heb. 10:24	Titus 2:7
Matt. 6:20	Luke 10:20	2 Cor. 5:1
1 Cor. 2:14	1 Cor. 1:18	Rom. 11:33

Scripture memory cards are available for $2.00 a set at Family Life Seminars, 2100 Greenfield Dr., El Cajon, Calif. 92021.

12

Summary

Well, that about winds it up. Now you realize you can study the Bible for yourself and that if you do, you will become a strong and effective Christian. What will it cost you? *Time*—or will it?

WHAT ARE WE
TALKING ABOUT IN TIME?

Earlier in the book I stated that there are four basic ways to study the Bible for yourself. The following formula will show the minimum time required to do each properly.

Daily Reading ✛ *Bible Stud*

15 Min. Daily	15 Min. Daily
	or
	30 Min. 3 Times
	Weekly

At first glance, 35 minutes a day (or 1/48th of a day) may seem like a lot of time from a busy schedule. But what would you think if I said it wouldn't take any time at all? That's right, it won't cost you one single minute—in the long run. Remember this, God is no man's debtor, that is, whatever we give God whether it is time, talent or money, He multiplies and gives it back to us. Many Bible verses teach this; for example, consider:

"But seek ye first the kingdom of God, and his righteousness, and all these things shall be added unto you" (Matthew 6:33).

"Give, and it shall be given unto you; good measure, pressed down, and shaken together, and running over, shall men give into your bosom. For with the same measure that ye measure it shall be measured to you again" (Luke 6:38).

A peculiar thing happens when we "honor God with the firstfruits" of our time through daily

+ *Learning*	**=***35 Minutes*
30 Min. Weekly and then spare moments daily	Daily or 4 Hours and 5 Minutes Weekly

Bible study. He so blesses and makes productive the remaining moments of our day that we don't miss it; in fact, we actually gain time. It amounts to this, 23½ hours blessed by God because we spent 35 minutes in His Word will be more productive than 24 hours without His blessing. Similarly, 4 hours a week spent in reading, studying and memorizing God's Word will so anoint the remaining 164 hours in your week that you will be more productive than you are in the 168 hour weeks when you neglect the Word of God. The God who multiplied the lad's lunch and fed 5,000 men is equally able to multiply our time when we give Him the first portion.

Once you learn God's system of economics and realize He is a multiplier of time, it won't be hard to be consistent in Bible study. For then you will have found the secret of time conservation.

A busy Sales Executive, when asked how he could afford to spend 35 minutes a day in Bible study replied, "I can't afford not to!" and neither can you!!

Daily Spiritual Diary

Week of _____ to _____

"I have desired the words of His mouth more than my necessary food."
Job 23:12

Sunday: Passage _____ Date _____
God's message to me today: _____
_____

A Promise from God   A Command to Keep   A Timeless Principle
_____   _____   _____
_____   _____   _____
_____   _____   _____

How does this apply to my life? _____
_____

Monday: Passage _____ Date _____
God's message to me today: _____
_____

A Promise from God   A Command to Keep   A Timeless Principle
_____   _____   _____
_____   _____   _____
_____   _____   _____

How does this apply to my life? _____
_____

Tuesday: Passage _____ Date _____
God's message to me today: _____
_____

A Promise from God   A Command to Keep   A Timeless Principle
_____   _____   _____
_____   _____   _____
_____   _____   _____

How does this apply to my life? _____
_____

Additional Comments _____
_____
_____
_____

Wednesday: Passage _____ Date _____

God's message to me today: _____

_____

A Promise from God	A Command to Keep	A Timeless Principle
_____	_____	_____
_____	_____	_____
_____	_____	_____

How does this apply to my life? _____

_____

Thursday: Passage _____ Date _____

God's message to me today: _____

_____

A Promise from God	A Command to Keep	A Timeless Principle
_____	_____	_____
_____	_____	_____
_____	_____	_____

How does this apply to my life? _____

_____

Friday: Passage _____ Date _____

God's message to me today: _____

_____

A Promise from God	A Command to Keep	A Timeless Principle
_____	_____	_____
_____	_____	_____
_____	_____	_____

How does this apply to my life? _____

_____

Saturday: Passage _____ Date _____

God's message to me today: _____

_____

A Promise from God	A Command to Keep	A Timeless Principle
_____	_____	_____
_____	_____	_____
_____	_____	_____

How does this apply to my life? _____

_____

Daily Spiritual Diary

Week of _____ to _____

"I have desired the words of His mouth more than my necessary food."
Job 23:12

Sunday: Passage _____ Date _____
God's message to me today: _____
_____

A Promise from God   A Command to Keep   A Timeless Principle
_____   _____   _____
_____   _____   _____
_____   _____   _____

How does this apply to my life? _____
_____

Monday: Passage _____ Date _____
God's message to me today: _____
_____

A Promise from God   A Command to Keep   A Timeless Principle
_____   _____   _____
_____   _____   _____
_____   _____   _____

How does this apply to my life? _____
_____

Tuesday: Passage _____ Date _____
God's message to me today: _____
_____

A Promise from God   A Command to Keep   A Timeless Principle
_____   _____   _____
_____   _____   _____
_____   _____   _____

How does this apply to my life? _____
_____

Additional Comments _____
_____
_____
_____

Wednesday: Passage _____ Date _____

God's message to me today: _____

_____

A Promise from God	A Command to Keep	A Timeless Principle
_____	_____	_____
_____	_____	_____
_____	_____	_____

How does this apply to my life? _____

_____

Thursday: Passage _____ Date _____

God's message to me today: _____

_____

A Promise from God	A Command to Keep	A Timeless Principle
_____	_____	_____
_____	_____	_____
_____	_____	_____

How does this apply to my life? _____

_____

Friday: Passage _____ Date _____

God's message to me today: _____

_____

A Promise from God	A Command to Keep	A Timeless Principle
_____	_____	_____
_____	_____	_____
_____	_____	_____

How does this apply to my life? _____

_____

Saturday: Passage _____ Date _____

God's message to me today: _____

_____

A Promise from God	A Command to Keep	A Timeless Principle
_____	_____	_____
_____	_____	_____
_____	_____	_____

How does this apply to my life? _____

_____

Daily Spiritual Diary

Week of _____ to _____

"I have desired the words of His mouth more than my necessary food."
Job 23:12

Sunday: Passage _____ Date _____
God's message to me today: _____
_____

A Promise from God	A Command to Keep	A Timeless Principle
_____	_____	_____
_____	_____	_____
_____	_____	_____

How does this apply to my life? _____
_____

Monday: Passage _____ Date _____
God's message to me today: _____
_____

A Promise from God	A Command to Keep	A Timeless Principle
_____	_____	_____
_____	_____	_____
_____	_____	_____

How does this apply to my life? _____
_____

Tuesday: Passage _____ Date _____
God's message to me today: _____
_____

A Promise from God	A Command to Keep	A Timeless Principle
_____	_____	_____
_____	_____	_____
_____	_____	_____

How does this apply to my life? _____
_____

Additional Comments _____
_____
_____
_____

Wednesday: Passage _____ Date _____

God's message to me today: _____
_____

A Promise from God	A Command to Keep	A Timeless Principle
_____	_____	_____
_____	_____	_____
_____	_____	_____

How does this apply to my life? _____
_____

Thursday: Passage _____ Date _____

God's message to me today: _____
_____

A Promise from God	A Command to Keep	A Timeless Principle
_____	_____	_____
_____	_____	_____
_____	_____	_____

How does this apply to my life? _____
_____

Friday: Passage _____ Date _____

God's message to me today: _____
_____

A Promise from God	A Command to Keep	A Timeless Principle
_____	_____	_____
_____	_____	_____
_____	_____	_____

How does this apply to my life? _____
_____

Saturday: Passage _____ Date _____

God's message to me today: _____
_____

A Promise from God	A Command to Keep	A Timeless Principle
_____	_____	_____
_____	_____	_____
_____	_____	_____

How does this apply to my life? _____
_____

Daily Spiritual Diary

Week of _____ to _____

"I have desired the words of His mouth more than my necessary food."
Job 23:12

Sunday: Passage _____ Date _____

God's message to me today: _____

_____

A Promise from God	A Command to Keep	A Timeless Principle
_____	_____	_____
_____	_____	_____
_____	_____	_____

How does this apply to my life? _____

_____

Monday: Passage _____ Date _____

God's message to me today: _____

_____

A Promise from God	A Command to Keep	A Timeless Principle
_____	_____	_____
_____	_____	_____
_____	_____	_____

How does this apply to my life? _____

_____

Tuesday: Passage _____ Date _____

God's message to me today: _____

_____

A Promise from God	A Command to Keep	A Timeless Principle
_____	_____	_____
_____	_____	_____
_____	_____	_____

How does this apply to my life? _____

_____

Additional Comments _____

_____

_____

_____

Wednesday: Passage _____ Date _____

God's message to me today: _____

_____

A Promise from God   A Command to Keep   A Timeless Principle

_____   _____   _____

_____   _____   _____

_____   _____   _____

How does this apply to my life? _____

_____

Thursday: Passage _____ Date _____

God's message to me today: _____

_____

A Promise from God   A Command to Keep   A Timeless Principle

_____   _____   _____

_____   _____   _____

_____   _____   _____

How does this apply to my life? _____

_____

Friday: Passage _____ Date _____

God's message to me today: _____

_____

A Promise from God   A Command to Keep   A Timeless Principle

_____   _____   _____

_____   _____   _____

_____   _____   _____

How does this apply to my life? _____

_____

Saturday: Passage _____ Date _____

God's message to me today: _____

_____

A Promise from God   A Command to Keep   A Timeless Principle

_____   _____   _____

_____   _____   _____

_____   _____   _____

How does this apply to my life? _____

_____

Book Study

Name of Book _____ How Many Times Read? _____

Date _____

1. Author _____
2. What were the circumstances of the author when written? _____
_____
_____

3. To whom written? _____
4. Tell something about them _____
_____

5. Where written? _____
6. When written? _____
7. Why was it written? _____
_____

8. What were the major problems? _____
_____
_____
_____

9. What solutions were given? _____
_____
_____
_____

10. What was the central meaning in that day? _____
_____
_____
_____

11. What is the central meaning today? _____
_____
_____
_____

12. Additional comments: _____
_____
_____
_____

Book Study

Book _____ Date _____

Summarize the main theme: _____
_____
_____
_____

Pick a key verse: _____
_____
_____
_____

Outline _____
_____
_____
_____
_____
_____
_____
_____
_____
_____
_____
_____
_____
_____
_____
_____
_____
_____
_____
_____
_____
_____

Book Study

Name of Book _____ How Many Times Read? _____

Date _____

1. Author _____
2. What were the circumstances of the author when written? _____
_____
_____
3. To whom written? _____
4. Tell something about them _____
_____
5. Where written? _____
6. When written? _____
7. Why was it written? _____
_____
8. What were the major problems? _____
_____
_____
_____
9. What solutions were given? _____
_____
_____
_____
10. What was the central meaning in that day? _____
_____
_____
_____
11. What is the central meaning today? _____
_____
_____
_____
12. Additional comments: _____
_____
_____
_____

Book Study

Book _____ Date _____

Summarize the main theme: _____
_____
_____
_____

Pick a key verse: _____
_____
_____
_____

Outline _____
_____
_____
_____
_____
_____
_____
_____
_____
_____
_____
_____
_____
_____
_____
_____
_____
_____
_____
_____
_____
_____

Book Study

Name of Book _____ How Many Times Read? _____

Date _____

1. Author _____

2. What were the circumstances of the author when written? _____

_____

_____

3. To whom written? _____

4. Tell something about them _____

_____

5. Where written? _____

6. When written? _____

7. Why was it written? _____

_____

8. What were the major problems? _____

_____

_____

_____

9. What solutions were given? _____

_____

_____

_____

10. What was the central meaning in that day? _____

_____

_____

_____

11. What is the central meaning today? _____

_____

_____

_____

12. Additional comments: _____

_____

_____

_____

Book Study

Book _____ Date _____

Summarize the main theme: _____
_____
_____
_____

Pick a key verse: _____
_____
_____
_____

Outline _____
_____
_____
_____
_____
_____
_____
_____
_____
_____
_____
_____
_____
_____
_____
_____
_____
_____
_____
_____
_____
_____
_____

Chapter Analysis

Passage _____ *Date* _____

1. What is the main subject? _____
_____
_____
_____

2. Who are the main people? _____
_____
_____

3. What does it say about Christ? _____
_____
_____
_____

4. What is the key or main verse? _____
_____
_____

5. What is the central lesson? _____
_____
_____

6. What are the main promises? _____
_____
_____
_____

7. What are the main commands? _____
_____
_____

8. What error should I avoid? _____
_____
_____

9. What example is here? _____
_____
_____

10. What do I need most in this chapter to apply to my life today? ___
_____
_____

Chapter Outline

Chapter _____ Date _____

Summarize the main subject: _____
_____
_____
_____
_____
_____
_____

Select the key verse: _____
_____
_____

Outline: _____
_____
_____
_____
_____
_____
_____
_____
_____
_____
_____
_____
_____
_____
_____
_____
_____
_____
_____

Chapter Analysis

Passage _____ *Date* _____

1. What is the main subject? _____
_____
_____
_____

2. Who are the main people? _____
_____
_____

3. What does it say about Christ? _____
_____
_____
_____

4. What is the key or main verse? _____
_____
_____

5. What is the central lesson? _____
_____
_____

6. What are the main promises? _____
_____
_____
_____

7. What are the main commands? _____
_____
_____

8. What error should I avoid? _____
_____
_____

9. What example is here? _____
_____
_____

10. What do I need most in this chapter to apply to my life today? ___
_____
_____

Chapter Outline

Chapter _____ Date _____

Summarize the main subject: _____
_____
_____
_____
_____
_____
_____

Select the key verse: _____
_____
_____

Outline: _____
_____
_____
_____
_____
_____
_____
_____
_____
_____
_____
_____
_____
_____
_____
_____
_____
_____
_____
_____

Bible Character Study

Character _____ Main Scripture Passage _____

Date _____

"These things happened unto them as examples unto us."

1. List other passages regarding his life. _____

_____

_____

2. Briefly describe his childhood, parents, family, education. _____

_____

_____

_____

3. What character traits do you see in him—good and bad? _____

_____

_____

_____

4. Describe his main encounter with God. _____

_____

_____

5. Who were his chief companions, were they a help or hindrance? _

_____

_____

_____

6. How did he influence others? _____

_____

_____

_____

7. What significant mistakes did he make? _____

_____

_____

(over)

© Copyright Family Life Seminars

8. Did he acknowledge and confess his sins? _____

9. What were his chief contributions in service to God? _____

10. Describe his family life. Was he a good parent? _____

11. How did his children turn out? _____

12. What is the primary lesson of his life that is profitable to you? ___

Bible Character Study

Character _____ *Main Scripture Passage* _____

Date _____

"These things happened unto them as examples unto us."

1. List other passages regarding his life. _____
_____
_____

2. Briefly describe his childhood, parents, family, education. _____
_____
_____
_____
_____

3. What character traits do you see in him—good and bad? _____
_____
_____
_____

4. Describe his main encounter with God. _____
_____
_____
_____

5. Who were his chief companions, were they a help or hindrance? _
_____
_____
_____
_____

6. How did he influence others? _____
_____
_____
_____
_____

7. What significant mistakes did he make? _____
_____
_____

Bible Character Study Pg. 2

_____

8. Did he acknowledge and confess his sins? _____

_____

_____

_____

9. What were his chief contributions in service to God? _____

_____

_____

_____

_____

10. Describe his family life. Was he a good parent? _____

_____

_____

_____

_____

11. How did his children turn out? _____

_____

_____

_____

_____

12. What is the primary lesson of his life that is profitable to you? ___

_____

_____

_____

_____

_____

_____

_____

_____

_____

© Copyright Family Life Seminars, 2100 Greenfield Drive, El Cajon, California 92021

Jesus' Life and Teachings

Passage _____ Date _____

1. Is the passage: About His life or teaching? _____
2. Give the essential details of the events. _____
_____
_____
_____

3. Who were His friends? _____
_____

4. Who were His enemies? _____
_____

5. Why were they opposed to Him? _____
_____

6. What other passages tell the same story? _____
_____
_____

7. What other details do they include? _____
_____
_____

8. What do you learn about His deity in this passage? _____
_____
_____

9. Everything Jesus did expressed the nature and attitude of God. What
did you learn about God in this passage? _____
_____
_____

10. What principles did He teach? _____
_____
_____
_____

11. What can you apply to your life? _____
_____
_____
_____

Jesus' Parables

Name of Parable _____

Passage _____ Date _____

1. What circumstances led up to this teaching, if any? _____

_____

_____

_____

2. Prepare a brief summary of the parable. _____

_____

_____

_____

_____

3. List any additional details given in parallel passages. _____

_____

_____

_____

_____

4. Does He give an interpretation? _____

_____

_____

_____

5. What is the one central truth He is teaching? _____

_____

_____

_____

6. Is there something here for me to apply to my life? If so, how can I do it? _____

_____

_____

_____

_____

_____

_____

Jesus' Life and Teachings

Passage _____ Date _____

1. Is the passage: About His life or teaching? _____
2. Give the essential details of the events. _____
_____
_____
_____

3. Who were His friends? _____
_____

4. Who were His enemies? _____
_____

5. Why were they opposed to Him? _____
_____

6. What other passages tell the same story? _____
_____
_____

7. What other details do they include? _____
_____
_____

8. What do you learn about His deity in this passage? ____
_____
_____

9. Everything Jesus did expressed the nature and attitude of God. What did you learn about God in this passage? _____
_____
_____

10. What principles did He teach? _____
_____
_____
_____

11. What can you apply to your life? _____
_____
_____
_____

Jesus' Parables

Name of Parable _____

Passage _____ *Date* _____

1. What circumstances led up to this teaching, if any? _____
_____
_____
_____

2. Prepare a brief summary of the parable. _____
_____
_____
_____

3. List any additional details given in parallel passages. _____
_____
_____
_____

4. Does He give an interpretation? _____
_____
_____
_____

5. What is the one central truth He is teaching? _____
_____
_____
_____

6. Is there something here for me to apply to my life? If so, how can I
do it? _____
_____
_____
_____
_____
_____

Psalms Study

Passage _____ *Date* _____

1. To whom is this Psalm addressed? _____
_____

2. List the blessings and the conditions for receiving them _____
_____
_____
_____

3. What promises did you find? _____
_____
_____
_____

4. Are there any commands? _____
_____

5. Is there anything that causes you to think particularly of Christ in this Psalm? _____
_____
_____
_____

6. What is the gist of the Psalm? _____
_____
_____
_____
_____

7. What central thought appeals to you? _____
_____
_____
_____
_____

8. What does this Psalm teach that you can do to be a happier or more blessed person? _____
_____
_____
_____

Psalms Study

Passage _____ *Date* _____

1. To whom is this Psalm addressed? _____
_____

2. List the blessings and the conditions for receiving them _____
_____
_____
_____

3. What promises did you find? _____
_____
_____
_____

4. Are there any commands? _____
_____
_____

5. Is there anything that causes you to think particularly of Christ in this Psalm? _____
_____
_____
_____

6. What is the gist of the Psalm? _____
_____
_____
_____
_____

7. What central thought appeals to you? _____
_____
_____
_____
_____

8. What does this Psalm teach that you can do to be a happier or more blessed person? _____
_____
_____
_____

Proverb Study

Proverb _____ *Date* _____

(The Proverbs were written to make man wise toward God and man.)

1. What is presented as wisdom? _____
   _____
   _____
   _____

2. What negatives are condemned? _____
   _____
   _____
   _____

3. What positives are commended? _____
   _____
   _____
   _____

4. List the timeless principles. _____
   _____
   _____
   _____
   _____

5. Do you know other passages that say the same basic thought? ___
   _____
   _____
   _____
   _____

6. Is there anything you have been doing that is here condemned? ___
   _____
   _____
   _____

7. Is there something taught here you need to incorporate into your daily life? _____
   _____
   _____
   _____

Proverb Study

Proverb _____ Date _____

(The Proverbs were written to make man wise toward God and man.)

1. What is presented as wisdom? _____
_____
_____
_____

2. What negatives are condemned? _____
_____
_____
_____

3. What positives are commended? _____
_____
_____
_____

4. List the timeless principles. _____
_____
_____
_____
_____

5. Do you know other passages that say the same basic thought? _____
_____
_____
_____
_____

6. Is there anything you have been doing that is here condemned? _____
_____
_____
_____

7. Is there something taught here you need to incorporate into your daily life? _____
_____
_____
_____

When Edmond and Jules Goncourt published the first part of their novel *Manette Salomon* in *Le Temps,* in January 1867, the two "sweeties" as Flaubert called them with fond irony, had been observing contemporary artists and collecting background information and notes for their book for a full two years. Their preparatory work took them to Fontainebleau, where they tasted the charms of rustic discomfort in the inns at Barbizon, and to Paris, into fashionable studios—they were intrigued by the oriental atmosphere that Tournemine had created—and to the Jewish quarters of the capital where many of the artists' models came from, including Manette herself. Although the brothers were notoriously misogynous and the novel is primarily the description of a man slowly dragged down by his love for a woman—the painter Coriolis besotted by the overwhelmingly beautiful Manette—it was, and still is, a precious record of life in the art scene in the mid-nineteenth century, because the Goncourts' meticulous research was well served by their talent for observation and their capacity for critical judgement. It fits into a long line of works stretching from Balzac's *Chef-d'œuvre inconnu* (1837) to Zola's *L'Œuvre* which gave artists and their work a central place in literature.

The novel was originally called *L'Atelier Langibout,* after the official studio where the young artists in the novel had been students—David's pupil, Drölling, was one of the sources for the character of Langibout. Indeed, the concept of the artist's studio itself is at the heart of the book. It was a place for working, teaching and entertaining and its size, arrangement, decoration and location were all clues to the owner's personality, his opinion of himself and the status he enjoyed in the art world of the mid-nineteenth century. The Goncourts thus distinguished the studio used by Langibout, a master with many students—"Langibout's studio was huge and painted olive green. The turntable stood against one wall [...]"[1]—from that of the likeable, lazy Anatole—"A studio reeking of poverty and youth, a hopeful attic, the studio in the Rue Lafayette, a garret with a good smell of tobacco and indolence!"[2]

Similarly, there was no common measure between the room bubbling with life and inspiration that was Coriolis' studio when he came back from the Middle East—"The studio was nine metres long and seven wide. Its four walls looked like a museum and Pandemonium. A disorderly array of baroque luxury, heaps of bizarre objects, exotic odds and ends, souvenirs and pieces of art [...]"[3]—and Garnotelle's orderly, tidy, dignified studio in the bourgeois Impasse Frochot—"Everything was neat and tidy, wiped clean, even the plants seemed brushed. Nothing was left lying about, not a sketch or a plaster, not a copy or a brush. It was an elegant art room [...]".[4] Visiting a studio meant meeting the artist himself, being invited into the inner recesses of his world—whether garret, museum or elegant art room—and divining the secrets of his art.

It is this artistic environment, in its very diversity—with its bare walls or jumble of plaster casts, prints and snapshots, comfortably furnished or stripped of everything but the easel, a meeting place or secret hideaway—which emerges in these photographs from the Musée d'Orsay. Collected since the late 1970s, many come from the papers of the artists themselves: the Bonnuit photographs come from the albums of a family of painters who worked at the Sèvres porcelain factory; others come from the Gérôme papers, the studio records of the cabinetmaker and sculptor François Carabin, the studio of the painter Mucha or that of Émile Gallé; still others were taken by Pierre Bonnard and Émile Bernard. There are few official portraits among them—and yet portraits of artists were a genre popularised by visiting cards, also known as "album cards" because they were later stuck into an album, as Alexandre Dumas complained, irritated to see himself "pinned like a butterfly in a display case". The choice here has deliberately focused on sensitive portraits, in which the photographer (named or anonymous) has tried to catch the inner world of the model. Portraits of artists by artists, these photographs are part of a tradition of shared representation which goes back to the Renaissance. The model and the photographer together create a scene which often emphasises friendship, as in Gustave Le Gray's photographs taken in Gérôme's studio in 1848 or Ponton d'Amécourt's shot of Victor Prouvé sitting in his studio in Nancy; or a young artist's respect for the man he acknowledges as his master, as in Émile Bernard's snaps in Cézanne's studio in Aix-en-Provence or Bonnard's shot in Rodin's studio; or again, familiarity with an environment, as in the photographs that Henri Sauvaire took in Camille Rogier's studio in Beirut or the anonymous photos of the painter Forain in the studio of his friend, the sculptor Geoffroy de Ruillé. Unfortunately, the collection does not include any of the group shots, taken in private studios or at the École des Beaux-Arts, which showed a crowd of unruly, dishevelled art students in a feverish hubbub around the turntable.

Gustave Le Gray and Jean–Léon Gérôme met early in the 1840s in the studio of the painter Paul Delaroche. They became fast friends—in 1848, Le Gray made a daguerreotype of a painting that Gérôme had entered in the Salon not long before: *Anacreon, Bacchus and Love*; the masterly reproduction marked the debut of both young men in the art world. The two pieces shown here (cat. 2 and 3) come from a set of photographs and manuscripts linked to the studios of Gérôme and his son-in-law, Louis-Aimé Morot. No doubt taken at Le Chalet, the communal studio that Gérôme shared with two fellow students, Hamon and Picou, rue de Fleurus, the two pictures emphasise the gaiety and joyful comradeship that prevailed in the studios of young artists at the time of the 1848 revolution, which many of these young Bohemians hoped would bring new freedom. Le Gray's talent and perfect mastery of exposure time and lighting has let nothing escape of the boyish enthusiasm for a summer afternoon in the studio courtyard. He has perfectly rendered their playfulness and vivacity and their pleasure at being together. The same gaiety infuses the photographs that Le Gray took in the courtyard of his own studio at the Clichy tollgate, a few years later. The mood is the same; so in photographing his friend's studio, he had tried to bring out not only the fervent, creative atmosphere of the place, but also that of his own studio, combining the two in a sort of friendly tribute.

In Beirut, in the mid-1860s, a diplomat and very talented amateur photographer called Henri Sauvaire (cat. 8 and 9) took a number of views of the salon-cum-studio, where Camille Rogier painted and entertained the social and artistic elite of the Phoenician city, then an obligatory and favourite stopping place for French travellers. Flaubert called in there in 1850 in the course of his voyage with Maxime du Camp and described it in a letter to his mother: "We have come across a very pleasant little group: the consul and his family, the French medical health officer, the chancellor, and the head of the post office, Camille Rogier, a decent painter stranded here who spends his time (thanks to the post office) orientalising in this beautiful country. We found ourselves in the same artistic set as Rogier. […] In short, it was a stroke of luck for us to be suddenly in a real artist's studio, where we picked up heaps of things—drawings, information and experience—that we would not have encountered elsewhere."[5] A friend of Théophile Gautier and Nerval, Rogier was a painter and illustrator who had yielded to the call of the Orient and settled in Beirut in the 1840s. Admired in the 1830s for his illustrations of *The Tales of Hoffmann,* he seems, as Flaubert ironically remarked, to have kept nothing of the painter during his Lebanese years but the look, the dress and the décor, failing the talent. Sauvaire has caught the welcoming atmosphere of the studio where the master of the house can be seen entertaining his guests as an artist, in oriental costume, in front of a blank canvas. The beautiful dark-haired woman leaning on the window sill, a picture of dreamy grace, perhaps posed for the photographer alone, since the painter seems unaware of her as a lovely visitor whose presence heightened the artistic feel of the studio.

Achille Bonnuit, a porcelain painter at the Sèvres factory, and his father-in-law Gérard Derischweiler both belonged to a small group of artists led by Louis Robert and Victor Régnault during the Second Empire who practised amateur photography with talent and skill. The Musée d'Orsay has five albums that once belonged to the family of Elisa Le Guay, who were painters at the Sèvres factory. The photographs in these albums reflect the artistic milieu of their authors; they are pictorial scenes, similar in tone to the canvases that Monet was working on at the time, in which the models can be seen posing in the woods near Sèvres. Several show a close-knit, joyous group of painters and decorators on the steps of the porcelain factory (cat. 10).

In the mid-nineteenth century, artists began to emerge from their studios. Like the Goncourts' painter Crescent—who was modelled on Théodore Rousseau and Millet—many decided to work in the open air. Nature doubled up as subject and workplace, the studio could be shifted to suit the chosen viewpoint; by breaking out of its walls, the studio was confounded with the subject of the painting. The painter Théophile Chauvel moved to Barbizon in the late 1840s. Several photographs in the collection of models for artists that he compiled show him in the forest near the places he liked to paint (cat. 12). Corot was acknowledged as a master and a precursor by many of these open-air painters. Charles Desavary's photograph, which shows him painting outdoors near Arras at the very end of his life, is as much a portrait as a manifesto (cat. 11). The scene became a conventional model for a portrait of an artist; Courbet had himself photographed in this way several times, having set up his easel in the countryside. The photographs in the Popelin albums showing an artist painting in the grounds of the family estate combine spontaneity and a sense of composition. As a counterpoint, another print from the same collection, showing a photographer who has hauled his heavy dark-room out of his studio and set it up on the quay, emphasises the equipment required for photography at the time and the care with which Daguerre's followers, like any painter, chose their viewpoints and the scenes they wished to represent (cat. 14). In 1906, the animal sculptor Rembrandt Bugatti moved to Antwerp, not far from the zoo. Wanting to observe the animals more closely, he set up his turntable near the cages and shaped plastiline models directly from the animals moving about before his eyes (cat. 28).

Many of the works in the exhibition record friendships between artists. The painter Forain, a friend of Verlaine's, poses with his wife, Jeanne Bosc, in the studio of the sculptor Geoffroy de Ruillé (cat. 15). The photographs that Émile Bernard took when he visited Cézanne in Aix in 1904 bring out the bare, rough, almost rugged look of the artist's studio: "[Cézanne] finally took me into his own workroom, amid his paintings; it was a large room, painted with grey tempera, with north lighting" (Émile Bernard, *Souvenirs sur Paul Cézanne et lettres*, Paris, 1924, p. 29). Like his fellow members of the Nabi group, Bernard was full of boundless admiration for Cézanne. He shyly asked permission to take some photographs. Cézanne allowed him to take two, in the studio with the *Large Bathers*—"On the mechanical easel he had just had installed, there was still a large canvas of nude women bathing, which was completely topsy-turvy. The drawing looked rather deformed to me. I asked Cézanne why he did not use models to do his nudes. He answered that at his age, a man ought not to undress a woman to paint her [...]" (cat. 25). There is no pretence in his portrait of the painter he so admired; he shows an artist exiled far from Paris where he was still misunderstood. Bernard had come to see him as a disciple, not to pay a social call. In the same way, Bonnard decided to photograph Auguste Rodin busy working on a bust of his friend, the sculptor Falguière (cat. 20). The painter has positioned him face-to-face with his work; the studio is scarcely visible; attention is focused on the artist who seems unaware of the spectator. The portrait of Emmanuel Frémiet by Stewart belongs to a different genre: it shows the sculptor at the end of his life and is meant as a homage to the artist. Frémiet is in a rather stiff, starchy pose. The size of the studio can be guessed from the height of the walls, which are adorned with sketches and drawings. It is the studio of a successful artist, in which he can give the measure of his talent (cat. 17).

Steichen photographed Henri Matisse as a sculptor in 1913. Matisse put great store by his sculpture. Far from being a derivative of his painting, it was an anchor point. He confided: "I am like Antaeus; I have to touch the earth from time to time". By creating a dialogue in counterpoint between the artist and his work, Matisse looking at the spectator, the sculpted woman turning her back on him, the artist in the light, the figure in the gloom, the blurred shapes of the artist's white smock, the sharp lines of the sculpture brought out by the photograph, Steichen pays homage to the artist's talent, revealing a lesser known aspect of his oeuvre (cat. 29), and one that lends itself more easily to black-and-white photography than the Fauvist's violent colours would have done. So sculptors' studios were a favourite setting for photographers wanting to recreate the close link between the sculptor and his work, which is based on hand movements, a succession of planes hollowed by the light to bring out the sculptures, and the subtlety of the shadows which is undiminished by the lack of colour. Shortly before World War I, Henri Manuel and his brother opened one of the great Paris studios and photographed several sculptors (cat. 27).

The studio was also the setting for the special, close relationship that developed between the artist and his model. The model was reality, living flesh. As the Goncourts put it, "the monopolising of attention by the life posing there before his eyes, the almost intoxicating effort to follow it closely, the passionate, desperate struggle of the artist's hand against visible reality".[6] The study of a live model was the crucial last stage in an artist's training in the nineteenth century. Although only male models were admitted to the École des Beaux-Arts—it was not until the 1880s that female models entered that venerable institution—women had been posing for years in private studios, first for the masters and later in their pupils' studios. The poses they took were often inspired by the ancient sculptures used for academic teaching. The very beautiful nude by Charles Nègre blends the rigour and distance of an artist's study with an unrestrained pose (cat. 34). From the early days of photography, a complex relationship developed between the new invention and the nude, and the female nude in particular, a disturbing relationship playing on the seductive duality of the naked body and the academic figure used to train artists. As Ernest Bersot, the author of the article on the "Academy Figure" in *La Grande Encyclopédie,* wrote in 1890: "The nude, which is an essential grounding for the arts of drawing, sculpture and painting, would be shameful in photography." The daguerreotype, a unique object associated with private enjoyment, underlines this duality. The development of prints on paper in the early 1850s permitted wider distribution of "studies from the nude", supposedly academic figures for artists. Several of Igout's photographs came to the Musée d'Orsay with the Chauvel collection. Louis Igout specialised in academic nudes—men, women and children—and in studies of details—hands, feet, arms—and facial expressions. His work is academic and similar to the lithographed poses used in drawing classes (cat. 40).

The museum holds the stock of several studios; the artists often took the photographs themselves, or at least designed and arranged the poses. One of the most striking examples is an album of some thirty prints, taken in the 1870s, which no doubt belonged to an Orientalist painter (cat. 35–37). Three girls, sometimes together but often alone, pose in a spacious studio hung with drapes and furnished with a divan covered with carpets to suggest an oriental interior. The scenes, as is often the case in paintings evoking the mythical Orient where every woman is an odalisque, combine conventional poses and seductive attitudes. One of the most original shows a girl stretched out on the rugs playfully embraced by a plaster mask, a studio prop that she is flirting with. The most intriguing of all is no doubt the album that once belonged to the painter Charles Jeandel (cat. 41 and 42). An obscure artist—until recent research by Hélène Pinet—and a student at the Jullian Academy, he was mentioned only once in the catalogue of the Salon des artistes français in 1883, with *Overturning the Idol of Serapis.* His weird album contains a few family photographs, five or six landscapes, and a squared church scene, alongside tens of photographs of naked women bound to the beams in the artist's studio in the Rue de Douai, made even stranger by the use of cyanotypes, blue prints which give a remote effect. The studio is large but plain and the idol of Serapis sometimes looms up in the background. As Hélène Pinet explains, Jeandel's studio is not "the huge, richly furnished studio of a painter at the peak of his career, but it is not the squalid studio of an artist crying poverty either." A provincial who had not been a great success in Paris, a mediocre painter but one with a decent income and respectable position that enabled him to live reasonably well, Jeandel does not seem to have designed his album as a repertoire of models. His dangling, bound, bruised women, whose suffering or at least discomfort is often apparent, were more likely the result of the thrill of erotic creation that his status as an artist permitted him to indulge in the privacy of his studio.

The hundreds of photographs of nude women from the stock of the cabinetmaker and sculptor François Carabin, despite the erotically charged crudeness of their poses, are closely related to the artist's work in decorating furniture. The many girls who posed for Carabin did not always have the charm of his sculpted women or their voluptuous curves, but, no doubt put at ease by the artist and full of the banter of young models in Montmartre, they freely strike the same poses with a naturalness that shines through in the photographs (cat. 44 and 45). Carabin's photographs came to the museum with Le Corbusier's papers, because the artist's heirs had given them to the architect in 1953. Despite the abysmal quality of some of the prints, they make a rare set that gives insight into the use of photographs not only as models but as preliminary sketches for other works. Many of the views were not taken any further, but remained as projects or ideas.

One of the great riches of the Musée d'Orsay's collections is a set of photographs that served as models for a scene put together for a painting. The origin of these photographs, often linked to the artists themselves, makes them even more precious. Two photographs from the

Gérôme papers, taken outside, probably on the roof of the artist's studio, show a man in Greek or Oriental costume; in one, he has a rifle over his shoulder, in the pose of Gérôme's *Arnaut Officer*, dated 1855 (cat. 50). Gérôme's relationships with photography are complex and require further study; his attachment to detail and his desire for accuracy prompted him to use photography on several occasions. During his first journey to the Middle East in 1856, he was accompanied by the young sculptor Bartholdi, who, on Gérôme's request, photographed houses in Cairo, and their moucharabys appeared in several of his oriental paintings. The works in the Musée d'Orsay show how the painter recreated, under Parisian skies, an imaginary Orient cleverly arranged to suit the needs of his work.

In the 1860s, the painter Olivier Pichat made a speciality of scenes from the Napoleonic epic. *The Emperor at St Helena* won a prize at the Salon of 1868. A set of twenty-one photographs reproducing military and oriental scenes has survived. If he did not take the photographs himself, the painter certainly arranged these military scenes, without bloodshed, in which uniformed models mimed hand-to-hand combat and battle scenes. Great care is taken to make them look realistic. Setting aside the background to the scene, with its distinctly unmilitary courtyard, and the soldiers' matter-of-fact, painless deaths, the fighting seems real enough at first glance. One of the images has been squared, which suggests that it was used as a model for a painting (cat. 52). Pichat's photographs thus emphasise the fruitful relationship between academic history painting and photography. Seldom acknowledged by the artists themselves, this use of the medium helped nourish their obsession with making their paintings look true to life and achieving historical accuracy. Seen beside Pichat's prints, the five anonymous photographs, known as *Models for History Paintings,* raise a smile; the scenes are incongruous and the costumes are amateurish, more in line with preparations for the costume balls that were all the rage among art students than with models for academic painting. In a spacious studio draped with tapestries, there are several characters dressed in costumes suggesting ancient Egypt: pharaohs, Egyptian queens and priests (cat. 54 and 55). Were they art students just larking about, dressing up with a few models? Or was the artist trying out a few poses—declamatory stances reminiscent of a Punch and Judy show—and testing the costumes for a huge Egyptian scene he intended to paint?

Donated by the artist's son, the photographs of models posing for the décor of the Bosnia-Herzegovina pavilion at the Universal Exhibition of 1900, designed by the Czech painter Mucha, shows how the artist used photography to adjust the composition of his decors and the pose of his models. The final scene, which won a silver medal at the Exhibition, is very close to the photographed scene in its general arrangement and in the poses. Some of the photographs have been squared, which gives a hint to their later use. But when he painted the décor, Mucha gave free rein to his Art Nouveau style, and the flowing figures seem to blend into his colourful floral décor. There is a distinction between the overall composition of the scene and its stylistic treatment. Yet the attention paid to the model and her pose gives Mucha's photographs the charm of a sketch infused with fondness for the model (cat. 56 and 57). The Catalan painter José Maria Sert often used photography in his work. Over six hundred photographs, taken between 1900 and 1945, have survived (of which ten are in the Musée d'Orsay). In his studio, he photographed models in poses that he used in his frescoes for Vich cathedral, for example, or to decorate private houses. The power of the male models, the vigour of the movement, and the use of harsh lighting gives these photographic sketches great force (cat. 59 and 60). As Sylvie Aubenas points out, Sert's use of photographs as preparatory models brought him in touch with the tradition of Renaissance fresco painters. When Edgar Degas died, a hundred wax models of dancers or horses (studies of movement and torsion) were found in his studio in the Boulevard de Clichy. Although they were not intended for sale, Degas made no secret of them because he exhibited the wax model of *The Little Dancer, Aged Fourteen*. In 1897, he even told Thiébault-Sisson:

"The truth can be obtained only by a model, because it forces you not to overlook anything that counts". He added: "I made wax models of animals and people, for my own satisfaction, not to take a rest from my painting and drawings, but to give my paintings and drawings more expression, more ardour and life […]". These wax models, in which Degas's stubborn insistence on movement shows through with grace and emotion, were photographed in December 1917 in the painter's studio, shortly after his death, by a man named Gautier, probably on Vollard's request. Focusing on the figures themselves, the photographs show nothing of the studio, but provide a valuable, faithful record of the artist's work and his creative process (cat. 61 and 62). Sometimes placed on a few books to bring them up to the right height, the models are just as Degas made them, sometimes still tied to their stands for extra stability. Although some of them are in the Musée d'Orsay, thanks to the generosity of Paul Mellon, most of them are in American collections, especially in the National Gallery of Art in Washington, D.C.

The artist's studio remains a secret place where the strange alchemy of creation is played out between the artist and his work. Gustave Courbet's masterpiece, *The Artist's Studio,* subtitled *A True Allegory Concerning Seven Years of My Artistic Life,* which he exhibited in a private exhibition on the fringe of the Universal Exhibition in Paris in 1855, does not dispel the mystery, despite Courbet's stated intentions. "It is the physical and psychological history of my studio, part one," he wrote to Champfleury in January 1855. "These are the people who serve me, support me in my thinking, and participate in my action. These are the people who make a living from life and from death. […] In short, it is my way of seeing society through its interests and passions. These are the people who come to be painted in my studio." The painting has given rise to many pictorial, social, historical and political explanations. But despite Courbet's arrogant claim, is it really society that is depicted here? Surely it is in the centre of the canvas itself that we should look for the meaning of this picture, in the artist's gesture towards his painting, a gesture which underlines his attachment to the material nature of his art. The picture remains mysterious. An image of the close, constantly renewed bond between the artist and his oeuvre. The photographs exhibited here, though they obviously do not have the same scope as Courbet's huge canvas, reveal—but do not unveil—the creative world of the artists working in the second half of the nineteenth century.

Notes

1. Edmond et Jules de Goncourt, *Manette Salomon* (Paris: Gallimard, "Folio" coll.), p. 98.

2. *Ibid.*, p. 154.

3. *Ibid.*, p. 216.

4. *Ibid.*, p. 239.

5. Gustave Flaubert, "Letter to his mother on 9 August 1850", in *Correspondance,* Vol I (Paris: Gallimard, coll. "Bibliothèque de la Pléiade"), p. 660.

6. Edmond et Jules de Goncourt, *Manette Salomon* (see note 1), p. 179.

Entries

1. Robert J. Bingham (London ?, England, 1825 ? – Brussels, Belgium, 1870), *L'Atelier de Paul Delaroche* [Paul Delaroche's Studio], from an oil on canvas by Louis Roux, 1858, pl. 86 of the *Album des œuvres de Paul Delaroche reproduites en photographie par Robert Bingham*, published by Goupil et Cie. Albumen print from a glass negative, inscription on the mount lower right: "86/Atelier de Paul Delaroche peint par Louis Roux/publié par Goupil et Cie", 14.5 x 21 cm. Gift of the Kodak-Pathé Foundation.
PHO 1983 165 159 86

Paul Delaroche's studio was a gathering place for many artists in the mid-nineteenth century. Gérôme was one of his students and several others later became talented photographers: Gustave Le Gray, Charles Nègre and Henri Le Secq, to mention only the most famous. In 1858, Goupil published a portfolio of photographs by Robert Bingham of Paul Delaroche's entire oeuvre, either from the canvases themselves or from engravings. This portfolio was the first photographic reproduction of the work of a nineteenth-century artist.

2. Gustave Le Gray (Villiers-le-Bel, France, 1820 – Cairo, Egypt, 1884), *Groupe d'hommes et une femme assise sur un perron* [A Group of Men and a Woman Sitting on the Steps], 1848. Salted paper print from a paper negative, signed and dated lower right in black ink: "Gustave Le Gray, 1848", 10.9 x 13.9 cm.
PHO 2003 4 40

This photograph, probably taken in Le Chalet, the studio at 27 rue de Fleurus, near the Luxembourg Gardens in Paris that Jean-Léon Gérôme (1824–1904) shared with Jean-Louis Hamon (1821–1874) and Henri Picou (1824–1895) is from the collection of photographs that once belonged to Gérôme and his

son-in-law Louis-Aimé Morot (1850–1913) and has just been acquired by the Musée d'Orsay.

3. Gustave Le Gray (Villiers-le-Bel, France, 1820 – Cairo, Egypt, 1884), *Six hommes debout dans une cour, derrière un paravent* [Six Men in a Courtyard, Standing Behind a Screen], ca. 1848. Salted paper print from a paper negative, 16.5 x 20 cm.
PHO 2003 4 41

This photograph, like the previous one, is from the Gérôme-Morot collection and was probably also taken in the courtyard of Le Chalet.

4. Charles Nègre (Grasse, France, 1820 – 1880), *Le Photographe Henri Le Secq (1818–1881), une petite fille et un joueur d'orgue de barbarie dans la cour de l'atelier de Charles Nègre, 21 quai Bourbon, à Paris* [The Photographer Henri Le Secq (1818–1881), a Little Girl and an Organ Grinder in the Courtyard of Charles Nègre's Studio, 21 Quai Bourbon, Paris], ca. 1852. Dry waxed paper negative, 16.5 x 21.5 cm.
PHO 1999 2

Nègre's studio on the island of Saint-Louis, where many artists had studios at the time, was often the setting for his photographs in Paris.

5. Anonymous, *Honoré Daumier dans son atelier* [Honoré Daumier in his Studio], ca. 1850. Salted paper print from a paper negative, 12.3 x 9.5 cm. Gift of M. Baderou.
PHO 1982 104

From 1846 to 1862, Daumier had a studio at 9 Quai d'Anjou, on the Saint-Louis. He was an acute observer of contemporary manners and from 1841 to the late 1850s produced several caricatures on the subject of photography and the enthusiasm it sparked among the bourgeois.

6. Anonymous, *Honoré Daumier sur le toit de son atelier* [Honoré Daumier on the Roof of his Studio], ca. 1860. Albumen print from a glass negative, 9.8 x 6.1 cm.
PHO 2001 4
This photograph, taken on the roof of the studio on the Quai d'Anjou, belonged to the sculptor Adolphe Victor Geoffroy-Dechaume (1816–94), one of Daumier's close friends and most loyal supporters.

7. Louis Robert (Paris, France, 1811 – Sèvres, France, 1882), *Le Peintre Constant Troyon (1810–1865) dans son atelier du 21 rue Rochecourt* [The painter Constant Troyon (1810–1865) in his Studio at 21 Rue Rochecourt], ca. 1855, f. 60 of the Watelin de Lummen album. Salted paper print from a collodion-on-glass negative, 17.4 x 13.4 cm.
PHO 1984 98 28
Louis Robert, one of a family of painters at the Sèvres porcelain factory, became the head of the painting workshop in 1848 and then director of the factory from 1871 to 1878. He was a gifted amateur photographer and his group at Sèvres was one of the most active photography circles under the Second Empire.

8. Henri Sauvaire (Marseille, France, 1831 – Robernier, France, 1896), *Portrait de Camille Rogier (1810–1893) avec deux hommes et une femme dans son atelier de Beyrouth* [Portrait of Camille Rogier (1810–1893) with Two Men and a Woman in his Beirut Studio], between 1860 and 1866. Albumen print from a dry collodion glass negative, 12.4 x 17.4 cm. Gift of René and Bernard Sauvaire.
PHO 1995 33 130
Camille Rogier, a painter and vignettist, and a friend of Gautier and Nerval, was appointed director of the

French post office in Beirut in 1848. He continued his career as a painter alongside his official duties, using his studio to entertain the many French travellers who went through the Middle East.

9. Henri Sauvaire (Marseille, France, 1831 – Robernier, France, 1896), *Portrait d'une jeune femme dans l'atelier de Camille Rogier à Beyrouth* [Portrait of a Young Woman in Camille Rogier's Studio in Beirut], between 1860 and 1866. Albumen print from a dry collodion glass negative, 22.5 x 15.2 cm. Gift of René and Bernard Sauvaire.
PHO 1995 33 154
Henri Sauvaire was initiated into photography in France about 1855. He was familiar with the Middle East, where he had stayed several times, and was appointed chancellor of the French consulate in Beirut in 1864.

10. Achille Bonnuit (?, 1833 – ?, after 1894) and **Gérard Derischweiler** (?, 1822 – ?, after 1884), *Les Peintres de la Manufacture* [The Painters at the Sèvres Porcelain Factory], ca. 1860, in album 5, from a family of artists who worked at the Sèvres porcelain factory. Albumen print from a dry collodion negative, 15.2 x 11.8 cm.
PHO 1984 73 49
Achille Bonnuit, a gilder and decorator at the Sèvres porcelain factory, was part of the entourage of Louis Robert and one of the group of photographers who worked at Sèvres during the Second Empire. Derischweiler was his father-in-law. They can both be seen on the right in this picture.

11. Charles Paul Desavary (Arras, France, 1837 – 1885), *Camille Corot (1796–1875) peignant en plein air à Saint-Nicolas-les-Arras* [Camille Corot

(1796–1875) Painting Outdoors at Saint-Nicolas-les-Arras], 1871–1872. Albumen print from a glass negative, 14.2 x 10 cm.
PHO 1985 3

12. Anonymous, *Théophile Chauvel (1831–1909) devant le* Raphaël à *Fontainebleau* [Théophile Chauvel (1831–1909) in front of the Raphael at Fontainebleau], 1868. Albumen print from a glass negative, 19.5 x 25.4 cm. Gift of Marie-Thérèse and André Jammes.
PHO 1984 88 68

13. Gustave Popelin (Paris, France, 1859 – ?), *Une étude dans le parc, le Magnet* [A Study in the Park, Le Magnet], ca. 1890. Albumen print from a gelatine silver-bromide glass negative, 11.6 x 16.6 cm. Gift of Jean Soustiel.
PHO 1983 73 bis 29
Gustave Popelin belonged to the family of the painter Claudius Popelin (1825–1892), who knew the Goncourt brothers and was a friend of José Maria de Heredia. The Musée d'Orsay has several albums that once belonged to his family, depicting the life of official society artists during the Third Republic.

14. Gustave Popelin (Paris, France, 1859 – ?), *Le Photographe* [The Photographer], ca. 1890. Albumen print from a gelatine silver-bromide glass negative, 11.6 x 16.6 cm. Gift of Jean Soustiel.
PHO 1983 74 26

15. Anonymous, *Le Peintre Forain (1852–1931) et sa femme, née Jeanne Bosc, se regardant dans la glace dans l'atelier du sculpteur Geoffroy de Ruillé (1842–1922)* [The Painter Forain (1852–1931) and his Wife, née Jeanne Bosc, Looking at their Reflection in the Studio of the Sculptor Geoffroy de Ruillé (1842–1922), 1891. Albumen print, 22.5 x 16.9 cm.
PHO 1997 3 2
The painter and illustrator Forain, a friend of Monet and Degas, is seen here posing with his wife in the studio of the animal sculptor Geoffroy de Ruillé. Forain's caustic style made him a regular contributor to many magazines and newspapers in the late nineteenth century. Anti-Dreyfusard, like Degas, he produced several caricatures during the scandal that divided France.

16. Anonymous, *Jean-Léon Gérôme (1824–1904) travaillant au buste de Sarah Bernhardt* [Jean-Léon Gérôme (1824–1904) Working on the Bust of Sarah Bernhardt], ca. 1895. Albumen print, 11.9 x 16.6 cm.
PHO 2003 4 10
The Musée d'Orsay has the polychrome marble bust of Sarah Bernhardt (RF 1393). The plaster model is in the Tanenbaum collection in Toronto. The sculptor at work in his studio was the subject of several of Gérôme's paintings, especially *Pygmalion and Galatea* (Metropolitan Museum, New York), in which the artist brings his statue to life. After 1890, Gérôme quite often painted himself as a sculptor—several self portraits show him carving *A Woman Playing Bowls* or *Tanagra*.

17. William H. Stewart (? – ?), *Emmanuel Frémiet (1824–1910)* [Emmanuel Frémiet (1824–1910)], 1895, from the *Album de la deuxième exposition d'art photographique*. Photogravure covered with Japanese paper, 11.4 x 8.5 cm.
PHO 1991 15 51
A pupil of Rude and a gifted sculptor, Frémiet, whose animal statues are particularly remarkable, had a studio at 70 Rue de la Tour, Paris.

18. Ponton d'Amécourt, Vicomte de (? – ?), *Victor Prouvé dans son atelier (1858–1943)* [Victor Prouvé in his Studio (1858–1943)], 1898. Silver print from a gelatine silver-bromide glass negative, 22.5 x 15.8 cm. Gift of Marie-Thérèse and André Jammes.
PHO 1984 90

Victor Prouvé, a painter, sculptor and ornamenter, succeeded Émile Gallé at the head of the École de Nancy in 1904. This photograph was shown in 1898 at the Salon of the Lorraine Photographic Society of which Ponton d'Amécourt was an active member.

19. Anonymous, *Atelier de praticiens travaillant pour différents sculpteurs* [A Studio of Sculptors' Assistants], ca. 1893. Citrate print, 17 x 23.4 cm. Gift of Miss Godet.
PHO 1986 47

The Musée Rodin has a set of studio photographs from the papers of Henri Godet (1863–1937), a sculptor and a pupil of Mathurin Moreau.

20. Pierre Bonnard (Fontenay-aux-Roses, France, 1867 – Le Cannet, France, 1947), *Auguste Rodin (1840–1917) sculptant le buste de Falguière* [Auguste Rodin (1840–1917) Sculpting the Bust of Falguière], 1897. Albumen print from a flexible gelatine silver-bromide film, 9 x 6.5 cm. Gift, with a life interest, from the children of Mr and Mrs Charles Terrasse.
PHO 1987 28 74

21. Paul Haviland (Paris, France, 1880 – Yzeures-sur-Creuse, France, 1950), *Homme peignant dans son atelier* [A Man Painting in his Studio], ca. 1900. Silver print, 20.4 x 25.5 cm.
PHO 1993 1 136

Paul Haviland belongs to the great family of porcelain manufacturers from Limoges. His photographs in the early twentieth century were strongly influenced by the Pictorialist photographers and showed considerable talent. The Musée d'Orsay has a large collection of his prints and negatives.

22. James Craig Annan (Hamilton, Scotland, 1864 – Lenzie, England, 1946), *The Etching Printer, William Strang, Esq., A.R.A.*, [Le Graveur à l'eau forte, William Strang] ca. 1900, published in *Camera Work*, no. 19, plate II, 1907. Heliograph, 15.2 x 19.8 cm. Gift of Mina de Gunzburg through the Friends of the Musée d'Orsay.
PHO 1981 26 22

23. Anonymous, *Le Sculpteur Louis de Monard (1873–1939) avec* La Chasse de l'aigle [The sculptor Louis de Monard (1873–1939) with *An Eagle Attacking a Stallion*] 1906. Citrate print, 18 x 13 cm. Gift of Jacques Thomas.
PHO 1985 312

Louis de Monard studied sculpture with Froment. Here he is photographed in his studio in Bois-le-Roi. *An Eagle Attacking a Stallion,* inspired by a poem by Leconte de Lisle, is now in Bourges Town Hall.

24. Anonymous, *Bartholomé (1848–1928) dans son atelier* [Bartholomé (1848–1928) in his Studio], 1910. Silver print, 22.6 x 17 cm. Gift of Pierre Vitry.
PHO 1985 308

Paul-Albert Bartholomé is here shown in his studio in the Rue Raffet, Paris. Behind him rises the figure of *Glory* for the *Monument to Jean-Jacques Rousseau* in the Pantheon; its plaster model was exhibited at the Salon de la Société Nationale de Beaux-Arts in 1910. The monument was unveiled in the Pantheon on 30 June 1912.

25. Émile Bernard (Lille, France, 1868 – Paris, France, 1941), *Cézanne (1839–1906) assis dans son atelier, devant* Les Grandes Baigneuses [Cézanne (1839–1906) in his Studio, Sitting in Front of *The Large Bathers*], 1904. Silver print, 8.2 x 10.7 cm. Gift of the Friends of the Musée d'Orsay.
PHO 1994 42
The Large Bathers is now in the Barnes Foundation, Merion, Pennsylvania. In *Souvenirs sur Paul Cézanne et lettres*, published in 1924, Émile Bernard talks about visiting Cézanne in his studio in Aix in 1904, when this photo was taken.

26. Henri Manuel (Paris, France, 1874 – 1947), *Le Peintre Gervex (1852–1929) dans son atelier avec un modèle* [The Painter Gervex (1852–1929) in his Studio with a Model], ca. 1900. Gelatine silver-bromide glass negative, 23.7 x 17.8 cm.
PHO 1990 6 5

27. Henri Manuel (Paris, France, 1874 – 1947), *Bourdelle (1861–1929) dans son atelier avec un modèle* [Bourdelle (1861–1929) in his Studio with a Model], ca. 1900. Gelatine silver-bromide glass negative, 23.7 x 17.8 cm.
PHO 1990 6 16
The studio in the Impasse du Maine (present-day Rue Bourdelle) is now a museum dedicated to Bourdelle and his works. Bourdelle was a friend of Rodin's and worked as his assistant.

28. Anonymous, *Rembrandt Bugatti (1885–1916) modelant d'après nature au zoo d'Anvers* [Rembrandt Bugatti (1885–1916) Modelling from Life in Antwerp Zoo], 1906. Modern print from a gelatine silver-bromide negative on flexible film, 17.5 x 23.7 cm.
PHO 1985 309

Bugatti modelled from life with plastiline. In 1906, he moved to a studio on the Rempart des Béguines in Antwerp, with a view over the zoo which he visited every day.

29. Edward Steichen (Bivange, Luxembourg, 1879 – West Redding, Connecticut, USA, 1973), *Henri Matisse (1869–1954)* [Henri Matisse (1869–1954)], 1913, published in *Camera Work*, nos. 42–43, pl. VI, 1913. Photogravure, 22 x 17.4 cm. Gift of Minda de Gunzburg through the Friends of the Musée d'Orsay.
PHO 1981 32 15
Steichen photographed Rodin several times with *The Thinker* or the statue of Hugo. These photos are composed with clever use of chiaroscuro to make the sculpture loom up out of the shadows.

30. Anonymous, *Le Douanier Rousseau (1844–1910) peignant* Nègre attaqué par un jaguar [Henri Rousseau (1844–1910) painting *A Negro Attacked by a Jaguar*], 1910. Silver print, 11.8 x 16.2 cm.
PHO 1990 17 1
The painting *A Negro Attacked by a Jaguar* is now in the Kunst Museum, Basel.

31. Auguste Delaherche (Beauvais, France, 1857 – Paris, France, 1940), attributed to, *Les Sables rouges, les pots dans la cour* ["Les Sables Rouges", Pots in the Courtyard], 1901. Silver print, 10.5 x 8.5 cm. Gift of Mr and Mrs René Bureau.
PHO 1992 21 2 258
Auguste Delaherche, a decorator and ceramist, seems to have worked as an amateur photographer around 1900. The Musée d'Orsay has a large collection of photographs of his family, studio and models. His house and studio, "Les Sables Rouges", was at Armantières, near Beauvais.

32. Émile Gallé (Nancy, France, 1846 – 1904), attributed to, *Sur le verre, culture à la cristallerie de Gallé* [Plants Growing on Broken Glass at Gallé's Crystal Works], 1901. Silver print, on the print, lower right, an ink stamp: "Sur le verre cassé, culture à la verrerie de Gallé, 1901", handwritten in ink lower centre: "Atelier d'Émile Gallé à Nancy – Modèle et décor déposés n° 145", 15.8 x 21.5 cm. Gift of Mr and Mrs Jean Bourgogne. PHO 1986 6

33. Anonymous, *Une branche de fleurs d'orchidées* [A Spray of Orchid Flowers], ca. 1900, pl. 29 of Émile Gallé's collection of photographs. Citrate print, 22.5 x 16.2 cm. Gift of Mr and Mrs Jean Bourgogne. PHO 1986 71 29

Several photographic studies of flowers come from Émile Gallé's collection. The glass works had a charming study garden, a source of inspiration for floral decoration.

34. Charles Nègre (Grasse, France, 1820 – 1880), *Étude d'après nature, nu allongé sur un lit dans l'atelier de l'artiste* [Study from Life, a Nude Lying on a Bed in the Artist's Studio], ca. 1850. Waxed paper negative, 11.3 x 18.7 cm.

PHO 1981 4

The École Nationale des Beaux-Arts has another nude by Charles Nègre, probably taken in the same studio. Both shots show how the photographer combined culture and pictorial sensitivity with perfect mastery of photography on paper.

35. Anonymous, *Jeune Femme embrassée par un masque* [Young Woman Embraced by a Mask], ca. 1870, is from *Modèles dans un atelier de peintre orientaliste*. Albumen print from a glass negative, 19.5 x 16.2 cm.

PHO 1989 4 9

This photograph and the next two come from an album of thirty photos of models no doubt taken in the studio of an Orientalist painter, as the rugs and hangings suggest. The photographer, perhaps advised by the painter, has produced sensitive pictures in which the models still look natural and fresh despite their conventional poses.

36. Anonymous, *Deux jeunes filles nues* [Two Girls in the Nude], ca. 1870, from *Modèles dans un atelier de peintre orientaliste*. Albumen print from a glass negative, 21 x 16.3 cm.
PHO 1989 4 12

37. Anonymous, *Jeune Fille nue de profil* [Girl in the Nude from the Side], ca. 1870, from *Modèles dans un atelier de peintre orientaliste*. Albumen print from a glass negative, 21.3 x 17 cm.
PHO 1989 4 34

38. Wilhem von Gloeden (Mecklenburg, 1856 – Taormina, Italy, 1931), *Nu féminin*, about 1875 [Female Nude]. Albumen print from a glass negative, 22.5 x 17 cm.

PHO 1985 323 bis

The German photographer von Gloeden settled in Sicily in the 1880s. Attracted by the beauty of the young Sicilians, he took many photographs of boys and very young girls in a clearly erotic vein, although the quality of the lighting and composition is excellent. This photograph is much closer to a life study or an artist's model.

39. Pascal Sebah (? – Istanbul, Turkey, 1890), *Jeune Femme vêtue à l'orientale, un voile rayé sur les cheveux, au buste nu* [A Young Woman in Oriental Dress, with a Striped Veil over her Hair and Bare Breasts], ca. 1880. Albumen print from a glass negative, 21.5 x 15.9 cm.
PHO 1985 321

Pascal Sebah opened a photographic studio in Pera in 1857, then another in partnership with the photographer Polycarpe Joaillier, in Istanbul.

40. Louis Igout (Lyon, France, 1837 – after 1882), *Étude de nu, jeune femme alanguie sur une chaise* [Nude Study, a Young Woman Lounging on a Chair], ca. 1880. Albumen print from a glass negative, inscription on the negative, lower left: "E 107", 14 x 10.2 cm. Gift of Marie-Thérèse and André Jammes.
PHO 1984 88 1
This photograph belongs to the collection of the painter Théophile Chauvel. Igout sold his photographs—nude studies for artists—through the publishers Calavas or Giraudon. On the negatives, he wrote the letter 'E' for female nudes and 'F' for male nudes, followed by the number of the negative.

41. Charles-François Jeandel (Limoges, France, 1859 – Angoulême, France, 1942), *Femme à demi vêtue* [A Half-Dressed Woman], between 1890 and 1900. Cyanotype, 17 x 12 cm. Gift of the Braunschweig family in memory of the Texbraun gallery.
PHO 1987 18 73

42. Charles-François Jeandel (Limoges, France, 1859 – Angoulême, France, 1942), *Femme nue, trois-quarts dos, attachée* [Naked Woman, Three-quarter Back View, Bound], between 1890 and 1900. Cyanotype, 17 x 12 cm. Gift of the Braunschweig family in memory of the Texbraun gallery.
PHO 1987 18 91

43. Mario Marius Pictor (Bologna, Italy, 1853 – 1924), *Étude de nu dans l'atelier de l'artiste* [Nude Study in the Artist's Studio], ca. 1890. Albumen print from a gelatine silver-bromide glass negative, 12.5 x 8.5 cm. Gift of

Michele Falzone del Barbaro, in memory of the Texbraun gallery.
PHO 1987 13

44. François Rupert Carabin (Saverne, France, 1862 – Strasbourg, France, 1932), *Femme nue* [Nude Woman], ca. 1890. Citrate print, 10 x 6.2 cm.
PHO 1992 15 1 250
The sculptor and cabinetmaker Carabin took hundreds of photographs in his Montmartre studio.

45. François Rupert Carabin (Saverne, France, 1862 – Strasbourg, France, 1932), *Groupe de quatre femmes nues* [Group of Four Nude Women], ca. 1890. Citrate print, 12 x 17 cm.
PHO 1992 15 1 103

46. Émile Bernard (Lille, France, 1868 – Paris, France, 1941), *Deux modèles féminins dans l'atelier du peintre, l'un allongé, l'autre à genoux* [Two Female Nudes in the Painter's Studio, One Lying, the Other Kneeling], ca. 1910. Citrate print, 12.8 x 17.8 cm.
PHO 1997 11 2
This photograph comes from the studio records of the painter Émile Bernard.

47. Pierre Bonnard (Fontenay-aux-Roses, France, 1867 – Le Cannet, France, 1947), *Modèle retirant sa blouse dans l'atelier parisien de Bonnard* [Model Removing her Smock in Bonnard's Paris Studio], ca. 1910. Silver print, 8.2 x 5.8 cm.
PHO 1985 398

48. Robert Demachy (Saint-Germain-en-Laye, France, 1859 – Hennequeville, France, 1936), *Study (Étude)*, 1906, published in *Camera Work*, no. 16, pl. VI, 1906. Halftone from a gum bichromate print,

20 x 15.3 cm. Gift of Minda de Gunzburg through the Friends of the Musée d'Orsay.
PHO 1981 25 57

49. René Le Bègue (?, 1857 – ?, 1914), *Study (Étude)*, 1902, published in *Camera Work*, no. 16, pl. XI, 1906. Photogravure from a gum bichromate print, 21.8 x 11.7 cm. Gift of Minda de Gunzburg through the Friends of the Musée d'Orsay.
PHO 1981 25 62

50. Anonymous, *Modèle masculin vêtu à l'orientale, de face, un fusil sur l'épaule, sur le toit de l'atelier* [Male Model in Oriental Dress, from the Front, with a Gun over his Shoulder, on the Roof of the Studio], ca. 1855. Salted paper print from a paper negative, 20.7 x 14.5 cm.
PHO 2003 4 21
This photograph is part of the Gérôme-Morot collection. The pose is the same as that struck by Jean-Léon Gérôme's *Arnaut Officer*, in a private collection, Toronto.

51. Anonymous, *Modèle masculin vêtu à l'orientale, dans l'atelier* [Male Model in Oriental Dress, in the Studio], ca. 1870. Albumen print from a glass negative, 29.5 x 23.9 cm.
PHO 2003 4 6
This photograph is part of the Gérôme-Morot collection. Another print from the same group (PHO 2003 4 7) shows a female model, also in Oriental dress, in the same studio (Gérôme's perhaps).

52. Olivier Pichat (Paris, France, ca. 1825 – 1912), attributed to, *Deux militaires en joue* [Two Soldiers Taking Aim], ca. 1870, pl. 13 in *Vingt et une scènes militaires et orientalistes*. Albumen print from a glass negative, squared and numbered, 22 x 27.6 cm.
PHO 1993 9 13

Olivier Pichat painted many military scenes and exhibited several times in the Salons of the Second Empire (1864, 1868). This photograph and the following one come from his studio records. This print has been squared, according to a method used by artists since the Renaissance to avoid distortion when they were transferring painted sketches or drawings to a larger canvas. In the mid-nineteenth century it was used on photographs which, as here, served as preparatory studies for the finished work.

53. Olivier Pichat (Paris, France, ca. 1825 – 1912), attributed to, *Un soldat indigène debout de dos et un mort* [A Native Soldier Standing Up, Seen from the Back, and a Corpse], ca. 1870, pl. 15. in *Vingt et une scènes militaires et orientalistes*. Albumen print from a glass negative, 22 x 27.6 cm.
PHO 1993 9 15

54. Anonymous, *Trois personnes marchant en frise, costumées en pharaons* [Three People Walking in a Frieze, Dressed as Pharaohs], ca. 1880, from *Modèles de tableaux d'histoire*. Citrate print, 20.7 x 15.7 cm.
PHO 1985 315 2
This photograph and the following one belong to a set of five images probably used as models by a painter in the late nineteenth century.

55. Anonymous, *Trois personnages, un homme costumé en prêtre égyptien aux pieds d'une femme costumée en reine d'Égypte* [Three Characters, a Man Dressed as an Egyptian Priest at the Feet of a Woman Dressed as an Egyptian Queen], ca. 1880, from *Modèles de tableaux d'histoire*. Citrate print, 21.2 x 16.1 cm.
PHO 1985 315 4

56. Alphonse Mucha (Ivancice, Moravia, 1860 – Prague, Czechoslovakia, 1939), *Trois modèles masculins dans l'atelier de Mucha, devant le panneau central pour le pavillon de la Bosnie-Herzégovine de l'Exposition universelle de 1900 à Paris: la Bosnie offrant ses produits à l'exposition* [Three Male Models in Mucha's Studio, in front of the Central Panel for the Bosnia-Herzegovina Pavilion for the Universal Exhibition in Paris, 1900: Bosnia Offering its Produce to the Exhibition], ca. 1900. Citrate print, squared on the right side of the print, 18 x 13 cm. Gift of Jiri Mucha.
PHO 1979 77

57. Alphonse Mucha (Ivancice, Moravia, 1860 – Prague, Czechoslovakia, 1939), *Jeune Fille en prière: modèle dans l'atelier de Mucha devant* La Confirmation catholique*, frise supérieure du décor du pavillon de Bosnie-Herzégovine à l'Exposition universelle de 1900 à Paris* [Young Girl Praying: Model in Mucha's Studio in front of *Catholic Confirmation,* Upper Frieze from the Decoration for the Bosnia-Herzegovina Pavilion for the Universal Exhibition in Paris, 1900], ca. 1900. Citrate print, 18 x 13 cm. Gift of Jiri Mucha.
PHO 1979 78

58. Fernand Khnopff (Grembergen-lez-Termonde, Belgium, 1858 – Brussels, Belgium, 1921), *Marguerite Khnopff, sœur de l'artiste, étude pour* Le Secret *de 1902* [Marguerite Knopff, the Artist's Sister, Study for *The Secret,* 1902], ca. 1901. Citrate print, 15.5 x 11 cm.
PHO 2003 11
The Belgian symbolist painter Khnopff often used photographs without acknowledging them. His sister, who often posed for his paintings, was the main subject. The famous painting *Memories* which shows her from different angles and in various costumes is inspired by several photographs taken by Khnopff.

59. José Maria Sert y Badia (Barcelona, Spain, 1876 – 1945), *Étude de nu masculin* [Study of a Male Nude], ca. 1910. Silver print, 18.1 x 17.9 cm. Gift of the Michèle Chaumette gallery through the Friends of the Musée d'Orsay.
PHO 1991 19 1
This photograph is a study for the decoration of the drawing room of Chimenea Kent House, London. Sert used photography regularly after 1900. He made many photographic studies for the frescoes in Vich cathedral.

60. José Maria Sert y Badia (Barcelona, Spain, 1876 – 1945), *Couple* [A Couple], ca. 1910. Silver print, 23.3 x 17.3 cm. Gift of the Michèle Chaumette gallery through the Friends of the Musée d'Orsay.
PHO 1991 19 2

61. Gautier (active in Paris in 1917), «*Danseuse au repos les mains sur les reins, jambe droite en avant, deuxième étude*», *sculpture d'Edgar Degas* [Dancer at Rest, with her Hands on her Back, Right Leg Forward, Second Study, Sculpture of Edgar Degas], 1917, part of the Degas–Fèvre collection. Silver print, 19.4 x 7.1 cm. Gift of the Friends of the Musée d'Orsay.
PHO 1992 9 7
After Degas's death, Ambroise Vollard appears to have commissioned the photographer Gautier to prepare an inventory of his estate before the studio was sold.

62. Gautier (active in Paris in 1917), «*Femme surprise*», *sculpture d'Edgar Degas* [Woman Caught by Surprise, Sculpture by Edgar Degas], 1917, part of the Degas–Fèvre collection. Silver print, 15 x 7.8 cm. Gift of the Friends of the Musée d'Orsay.
PHO 1992 9 41

Selected Bibliography

AUBENAS, Sylvie, dir. *Le Photographe et son modèle, le nu au XIXᵉ siècl*. Paris: BNF / Hazan, 1997.

—, *Gustave Le Gray (1820–1884)*. Paris: BNF / Gallimard, 2002.

BAJAC, Quentin. "La photographie à Sèvres sous le Second Empire: du laboratoire au jardin". *48/14*, no. 5 (Autumn 1997), pp. 74–83.

—. *L'Invention de la photographie*. Paris: Gallimard, "Découvertes" coll., 2002.

BAJAC, Quentin, FONT-RÉAULX, Dominique (de), dir. *Le Daguerréotype français, un objet photographique*. Paris: Réunion des musées nationaux, 2003.

BALZAC, Honoré (de), preface by Adrien Goetz. *Le Chef-d'œuvre inconnu et autres textes*. Paris: Gallimard, "Folio" coll., 1996.

BATICLE, Jeanine, GEORGEL, Pierre. *L'Atelier: technique de la peinture*. Paris: Réunion des musées nationaux, "Les dossier du département des Peintures du Musée du Louvre" coll., no. 12, 1976.

BAUDELAIRE, Charles. *Écrits sur l'art*. Paris: Gallimard, "Folio" coll., 1972.

BILLETER, Erika. *Malerei und Fotografie im Dialog*. Zurich: Benteli, 1977.

CLARK, Kenneth. *Le Nu*. Paris: Hachette, "Pluriel" coll., 1987, 2 vols.

COMAR, Philippe. *Les Images du corps*. Paris: Gallimard, "Découvertes" coll., 1993.

DECKER, Sylviane (de). "Le Nu photographique, art impur, art réaliste". *Photographies*, no. 6, (December 1984).

GEORGEL, Pierre, LECOQ, Anne-Marie. *La Peinture dans la peinture*. Paris: Adam Biro, 1987.

GONCOURT, Edmond et Jules (de). *Manette Salomon*. Paris: Gallimard, "Folio" coll., 1989.

HOOG, Alain (d'), dir. *Autour du symbolisme, peinture et photographie au XIXᵉ siècle*. Brussels: Bozarbooks, 2004.

JOBERT, Barthélémy, dir. *Delacroix, le trait romantique*. Paris: BNF, 1998.

NÉAGU, Philippe, HEILBRUN, Françoise, MARBOT, Bernard. *L'Invention d'un regard*. Paris: Réunion des musées nationaux, 1989.

PAPET, Édouard, dir. *À fleur de peau, le moulage sur nature au XIXᵉ siècle*. Paris: Réunion des musées nationaux, 2001.

PEVSNER, Nikolaus. *Les Académies d'art*. Paris: G. Montfort, 1997.

PINET, Hélène. "Les photographies de Charles Jeandel: un si funeste désir". *48/14*, no. 16, (Spring 2003), pp. 84–93.

PINGEOT, Anne, DUREY, Philippe, dir. *La Sculpture française au XIXᵉ siècle*. Paris: Réunion des musées nationaux, 1986.

PINGEOT, Anne, LE NORMAND-ROMAIN, Antoinette. *Le Corps en morceaux*. Paris: Réunion des musées nationaux, 1989.

PINGEOT, Anne, HORVAT, Franck. *Degas sculpteur*. Paris: Imprimerie nationale / Réunion des musées nationaux, 1991.

POHLMANN, Ulrich. *Eine neue Kunst? Eine andere Natur! Fotografie und Malerei im 19. Jahrhundert*. Munich: Hypo-Kulturstiftung, 2004.

SCHARF, Aaron. *Art and Photography*. London: Penguin Books, 1989 (1ˢᵗ ed. 1968).

SCHWARTZ, Emmanuel, JACQUES, Annie. *Les Beaux-Arts, de l'Académie aux Quat'z'arts*. Paris: Ensba, 2001.

ZOLA, Émile. *L'Œuvre*, preface by Bruno Foucart. Paris: Gallimard, "Folio" coll., 1994.

Plates

1. Robert J. Bingham
L'Atelier de Paul Delaroche
1858

2. Gustave Le Gray
Groupe d'hommes et une femme
assis sur un perron
1848

3. Gustave Le Gray
Six hommes debout dans une cour,
derrière un paravent
Ca. 1848

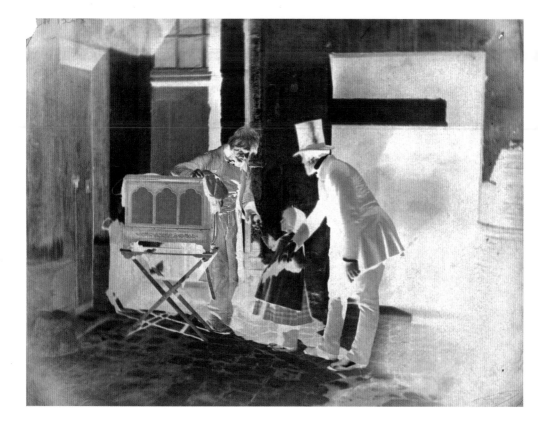

4. Charles Nègre

Le Photographe Henri Le Secq
(1818-1881), une petite fille
et un joueur d'orgue de barbarie
dans la cour de l'atelier de Charles
Nègre, 21 quai Bourbon, à Paris
Ca.1852

5. Anonyme
Honoré Daumier
dans son atelier
Ca. 1850

6. Anonyme
Honoré Daumier sur le toit de son atelier
Ca. 1860

8. Henri Sauvaire
Portrait de Camille Rogier (1810-1893)
avec deux hommes et une femme
dans son atelier de Beyrouth
1860/1866

9. Henri Sauvaire
Portrait d'une jeune femme
dans l'atelier de Camille Rogier
à Beyrouth
1860/1866

**10. Achille Bonnuit
et Gérard Derischweiler**
Les Peintres de la Manufacture
Ca. 1860

11. Charles Paul Desavary
*Camille Corot (1796-1875)
peignant en plein air
à Saint-Nicolas-les-Arras*
1871/1872

12. Anonyme
Théophile Chauvel (1831-1909)
devant le Raphaël à Fontainebleau
1868

13. Gustave Popelin
Une étude dans le parc, le Magnet
Ca. 1890

14. Gustave Popelin
Le Photographe
Ca. 1890

15. Anonyme
*Le Peintre Forain (1852-1931)
et sa femme, née Jeanne
Bosc, se regardant dans
la glace dans l'atelier
du sculpteur Geoffroy
de Ruillé (1842-1922)*
1891

16. Anonyme
Jean-Léon Gérôme (1824-1904)
travaillant au buste de Sarah Bernhardt
Ca. 1895

17. William H. Stewart
Emmanuel Frémiet
(1824-1910)
1895

18. Ponton d'Amécourt
Victor Prouvé dans son atelier
(1858-1943)
1898

19. Anonyme
*Atelier de praticiens travaillant
pour différents sculpteurs*
Ca. 1893

20. Pierre Bonnard
Auguste Rodin (1840-1917)
sculptant le buste de Falguière
1897

21. Paul Haviland
Homme peignant dans son atelier
Ca. 1900

22. James Craig Annan
Le Graveur à l'eau forte,
William Strang (The Etching Printer,
William Strang, Esq., A.R.A.)
Ca. 1900

23. Anonyme
Le Sculpteur Louis de Monard (1873-1939) avec La Chasse de l'aigle
1906

24. Anonyme
*Bartholomé (1848-1928)
dans son atelier*
1910

25. Émile Bernard
*Cézanne (1839-1906) assis dans son atelier,
devant* Les Grandes Baigneuses
1904

26. Henri Manuel
*Le Peintre Gervex
(1852-1929) dans son
atelier avec un modèle*
Ca.1900

27. Henri Manuel
Bourdelle (1861-1929)
dans son atelier avec un modèle
Ca. 1900

28. Anonyme
Rembrandt Bugatti (1885-1916)
modelant d'après nature au zoo d'Anvers
1906

29. Edward Steichen
Henri Matisse
(1869-1954)
1913

30. Anonyme
Le Douanier Rousseau (1844-1910)
peignant Nègre attaqué par un jaguar
1910

31. Auguste Delaherche, attribué à
Les Sables rouges,
les pots dans la cour
1901

32. Émile Gallé, attribué à
Sur le verre, culture à la cristallerie de Gallé
1901

33. Anonyme
Une branche de fleurs
d'orchidées
Ca. 1900

34. Charles Nègre
*Étude d'après nature, nu allongé
sur un lit dans l'atelier de l'artiste*
Ca. 1850

35. Anonyme
*Jeune Femme embrassée
par un masque*
Ca. 1870

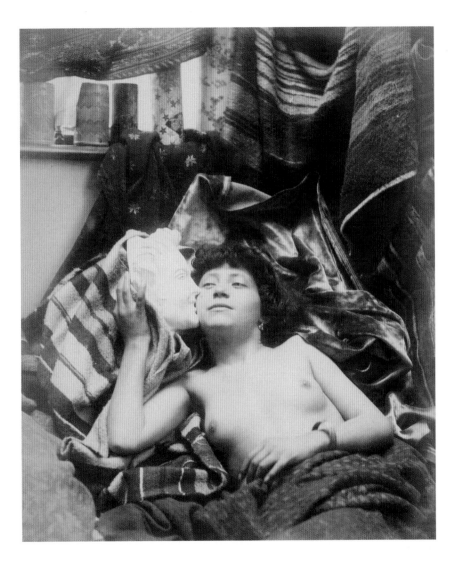

36. Anonyme
Deux jeunes filles nues
Ca. 1870

37. Anonyme
Jeune Fille nue de profil
Ca. 1870

38. Wilhem von Gloeden
Nu féminin
Ca. 1875

39. Pascal Sebah
Jeune Femme vêtue
à l'orientale, un voile
rayé sur les cheveux,
au buste nu
Ca. 1880

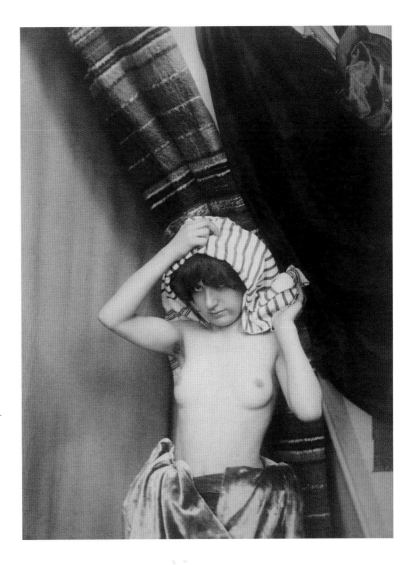

E. 107

40. Louis Igout
Étude de nu, jeune femme
alanguie sur une chaise
Ca. 1880

41. Charles-François Jeandel
Femme à demi vêtue
1890/1900

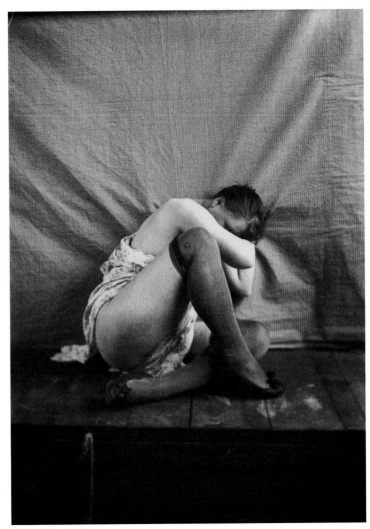

42. Charles-François Jeandel
Femme nue, de trois-quarts dos,
attachée
1890/1900

43. Mario Marius Pictor
Étude de nu dans l'atelier de l'artiste
Ca. 1890

44. François Rupert Carabin
Femme nue
Ca. 1890

45. François Rupert Carabin
Groupe de quatre femmes nues
Ca. 1890

46. Émile Bernard
*Deux modèles féminins dans l'atelier
du peintre, l'un allongé, l'autre à genoux*
Ca. 1910

47. Pierre Bonnard
Modèle retirant sa blouse
dans l'atelier parisien de Bonnard
Ca. 1910

48. Robert Demachy
Study (Étude)
1906

49. René Le Bègue
Study (Étude)
1902

50. Anonyme
*Modèle masculin vêtu à l'orientale,
de face, un fusil sur l'épaule,
sur le toit de l'atelier*
Ca. 1855

52. Olivier Pichat, attribué à
Deux militaires en joue
Ca. 1870

53. Olivier Pichat, attribué à
*Un soldat indigène debout
de dos et un mort*
Ca. 1870

54. Anonyme
Trois personnes marchant en frise, costumées en pharaons
Ca. 1880

55. Anonyme
Trois personnages,
un homme costumé
en prêtre égyptien
aux pieds d'une femme
costumée en reine
d'Égypte
Ca. 1880

56. Alphonse Mucha
*Trois modèles masculins
dans l'atelier de Mucha,
devant le panneau central
pour le pavillon de
la Bosnie-Herzégovine
de l'Exposition universelle
de 1900 à Paris : la Bosnie
offrant ses produits
à l'exposition*
Ca. 1900

57. Alphonse Mucha
Jeune Fille en prière : modèle
dans l'atelier de Mucha devant
La Confirmation catholique,
frise supérieure du décor du
pavillon de Bosnie-Herzégovine
à l'Exposition universelle
de 1900 à Paris
Ca. 1900

58. Fernand Khnopff
Marguerite Khnopff,
sœur de l'artiste, étude
pour Le Secret *de 1902*
Ca. 1901

59. José Maria Sert y Badia
Étude de nu masculin
Ca. 1910

60. José Maria Sert y Badia
Couple
Ca. 1910

61. Gautier
*«Danseuse au repos les mains
sur les reins, jambe droite en avant,
deuxième étude», sculpture
d'Edgar Degas*
1917

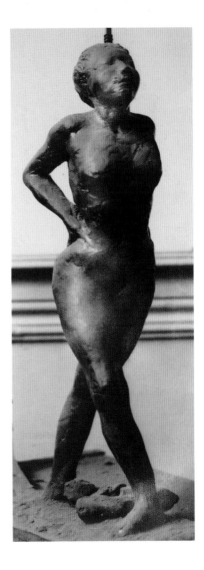

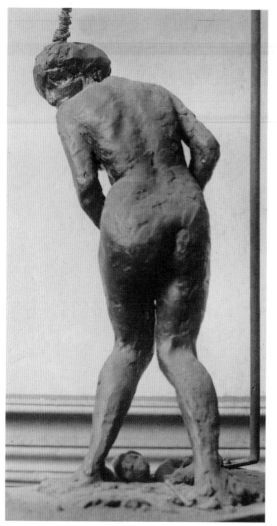

62. Gautier
« Femme surprise »,
sculpture d'Edgar Degas
1917